Samuel French Acting Edition

August Wilson's
Ma Rainey's
Black Bottom

SAMUELFRENCH.COM   SAMUELFRENCH.CO.UK

FOR PRODUCTION ENQUIRIES

UNITED STATES AND CANADA
Info@SamuelFrench.com
1-866-598-8449

UNITED KINGDOM AND EUROPE
Plays@SamuelFrench.co.uk
020-7255-4302

Each title is subject to availability from Samuel French, depending upon country of performance. Please be aware that *AUGUST WILSON'S MA RAINEY'S BLACK BOTTOM* may not be licensed by Samuel French in your territory. Professional and amateur producers should contact the nearest Samuel French office or licensing partner to verify availability.

MA RAINEY'S BLACK BOTTOM by August Wilson, opened at the Yale Repertory Theatre on April 6, 1984; directed by Lloyd Richards; settings designed by Charles Henry McClennahan; costumes designed by Daphne Pascucci; lighting designed by Peter Maradudin; musical direction by Dwight Andrews; stage managed by K. White; with the following cast:

STURDYVANT.............................. Richard M. Davidson
IRVIN ....Lou Criscuolo
CUTLER ....Joe Seneca
TOLEDO .... Robert Judd
SLOW DRAG...................................Leonard Jackson
LEVEE.......................................Charles S. Dutton
MA RAINEY....................................Theresa Merritt
POLICEMAN..............................David Wayne Nelson
DUSSIE MAE...................................Aleta Mitchell
SYLVESTER.....................................Steven R. Blye

MA RAINEY'S BLACK BOTTOM by August Wilson, opened at the Cort Theatre on October 11, 1984; directed by Lloyd Richards; settings designed by Charles Henry McClennahan; costumes designed by Daphne Pascucci; lighting designed by Peter Maradudin; musical direction by Dwight Andrews; stage managed by Mortimer Halpern; with the following cast:

STURDYVANT..................................John Carpenter
IRVIN ....Lou Criscuolo
CUTLER ....Joe Seneca
TOLEDO .... Robert Judd
SLOW DRAG...................................Leonard Jackson
LEVEE.......................................Charles S. Dutton
MA RAINEY....................................Theresa Merritt
DUSSIE MAE...................................Aleta Mitchell
SYLVESTER............................ Scott Davenport-Richards
POLICEMAN................................Christopher Loomis

Originally produced on the New York stage by Robert Cole, Ivan Bloch and Fred Zollo.

MUSIC USE NOTE

IMPORTANT BILLING AND CREDIT REQUIREMENTS

CHARACTERS

STURDYVANT

IRVIN

CUTLER

TOLEDO

SLOW DRAG

LEVEE

MA RAINEY

POLICEMAN

DUSSIE MAE

SYLVESTER

ACT ONE

*(Sound: A female vocal rendition of "C.C. Rider."
Lights: Fade to black, then after a moment, a
warm glow fades up in the front hall from the
overhead fixture spilling in through the double
door windows, creating a dim glow in the Studio,
and cool daylight fades up, streaming through the
dirty casement window in the Bandroom. Sound:
The song ends.)*

*(**STURDYVANT** enters down the Front Hall
carrying a small bundle, followed by **IRVIN**.
STURDYVANT flips a light switch left of the double
doors. [Lights: The overhead practicals go on,
generally illuminating the studio.] **STURDYVANT**
quickly surveys the studio, moves toward the spiral
staircase and finds his path blocked by the wooden
stool. He moves the stool toward the right wall and
starts to climb the staircase as **IRVIN** crosses to the
radiator. **IRVIN** shivers, touches the radiator and
turns the valve. **STURDYVANT** reaches the top of
the staircase, opens the control booth door and flips
a switch just inside the door.)*

*([Lights: The lamps come on in the Control
Booth and the stairwell of the spiral staircase.]
STURDYVANT unwraps the bundle revealing
recording discs, which he begins to examine as
IRVIN crosses to the singer's platform, picks up the
music stand, moves the cane chair off the platform
to the right, and crosses to the left door. **IRVIN** opens
the door, exits into the back hall and disappears
into a closet to the right.)*

([Lights: The closet light comes up, dimly illuminating the back hall and a descending step to the left.] **IRVIN** *returns carrying a microphone with a coiled cable on a tall stand. He places it in the center of the singer's platform, uncoils the mic cable, plugs it into the upstage left jack box, then returns to the mic.* **IRVIN** *cranes his neck to blow into mic, taps it a few times, glances up to the control booth, shrugs his shoulders, then crosses to the piano as* **STURDYVANT** *looks up and puts on his headphones.* **IRVIN** *reaches for the piano keys.)*

STURDYVANT. *(Speaks into the control booth microphone and is heard over speaker horn in the Studio.)* Irv...let's check that mic, huh?

*(***IRVIN*** steps away from the piano, points at the mic and nods his head. Into the booth mic:)*

Let's do a check on it.

IRVIN. *(Sighs, crosses to the mic and speaks into it.)* Testing... One... Two... Three...

([Sound: A piercing squeal of feedback over the horn speaker.] **IRVIN** *covers his ears in pain and glares at* **STURDYVANT.** **STURDYVANT** *turns upstage and adjusts the dials on the mixer.* **IRVIN** *speaks into the mic again. Cautiously:)*

Testing... One... Two... Three... Testing...

*(***STURDYVANT*** takes off his headphones and examines the recording discs.)*

How's that, Mel? *(***IRVIN*** pauses, then continues loudly.)* Testing... One... Two...

STURDYVANT. *(Looks at* **IRVIN,** *hastily, into the booth mic:)* Okay...that checks. We got a good reading.

*(***IRVIN*** crosses to the music stand upstage right. Into the booth mic:)*

You got that list, Irv?

IRVIN. *(Picks up the music stand and crosses toward the left door.)* Yeah...yeah I got it. Don't worry about nothing. *(Exits through the left doorway and into the closet.)*

STURDYVANT. *(Into the booth mic.)* Listen, Irv...you keep her in line, okay? *(IRVIN returns, crosses to downstage right of the piano and looks at STURDYVANT. Into the booth mic:)* I'm holding you responsible for her...if she starts any of her...

IRVIN. Mel...what's with the goddamn horn? You wanna talk to me...okay! I can't talk to you over the goddamn horn...christ!

STURDYVANT. *(Into the booth mic.)* I'm not putting up with any of her shenanigans. You hear? Irv?

> *(IRVIN crosses to the piano and bangs on the keys. STURDYVANT tries to yell over the cacophony, into the booth mic.)*

I'm just not gonna stand for it. I want you to keep her in line. Irv? *(STURDYVANT leaves the control booth, bounds down the spiral staircase and lands right of IRVIN. IRVIN stops pounding the piano keys.)* Listen, Irv...you're her manager...she's your responsibility...

IRVIN. *(Crosses below STURDYVANT to the double doors.)* Okay, okay, Mel...let me handle it.

STURDYVANT. *(Fuming.)* She's your responsibility. I'm not putting up with any of this Royal Highness... Queen of the Blues bullshit!

IRVIN. *(Humorously.)* Mother of the Blues, Mel. Mother of the *Blues.* *(IRVIN opens the upstage side of the double doors and goes into the Front Hall.)*

STURDYVANT. *(He crosses to the double doors, grabs the door and holds it open. IRVIN hangs his hat and coat on the wall hooks.)* I don't care what she calls herself. I'm not putting up with it. I just want to get her in here... record those songs on that list...and get her out. Just like clockwork, huh?

IRVIN. *(Crosses through the open door to left of* **STURDYVANT.***)* Like clockwork, Mel. You just stay out of the way and let me handle it.

STURDYVANT. *(Lets the door swing shut, crosses to the radiator and turns the valve, as* **IRVIN** *picks up two of the wooden folding chairs and crosses toward the singer's platform.)* Yeah…yeah…you handled it last time.

> *(***IRVIN** *unfolds one chair and places it upstage left of the platform.)*

Remember? She marches in here like she owns the damn place…doesn't like the songs we picked out… says her throat is sore…doesn't want to do more than one take…

IRVIN. *(Unfolds the other chair and sets it upstage right of the platform, over the mic cable.)* Okay…okay… I was here! I know all about it.

STURDYVANT. *(He crosses below* **IRVIN** *to the microphone as* **IRVIN** *counters to the radiator.* **STURDYVANT** *lowers the mic stand to its lowest position, moves it to the left edge of the platform. He lifts the left folding chair, picks up the mic cable and reroutes it to left of the left folding chair.)* Complains about the building being cold…and then…trips over the mic wire and threatens to sue me. That's taking care of it?

IRVIN. *(Touches the radiator and turns the valve.)* I've got it all worked out this time. I talked with her last night. Her throat is fine…we went over the songs together… I got everything straight, Mel. *(Crosses to right of* **STURDYVANT.***)*

STURDYVANT. Irv, that hornplayer…the one who gave me those songs… Is he going to be here?

IRVIN. Yeah.

STURDYVANT. Good. I want to hear more of that sound. Times are changing. This is a tricky business now. We've got to jazz it up…put in something different. You know, something wild…with a lot of rhythm.

> *(***IRVIN** *looks at him blankly.)*

STURDYVANT. You know what we put out last time, Irv? We put out garbage last time.

> *(IRVIN crosses to the left door and exits right into closet as STURDYVANT straightens the folding chairs.)*

It was garbage. I don't even know why I bother with this anymore.

IRVIN. *(Returns from the closet carrying a crate of empty Coke bottles and crosses toward the double doors.)* You did alright last time, Mel. Not as good as before, but you did alright.

STURDYVANT. You know how many records we sold in New York? You wanna see the sheet? And you know what's in New York, Irv? Harlem.

> *(IRVIN opens the upstage side of the double doors, crosses into the Front Hall and the door swings shut. STURDYVANT shouts.)*

Harlem's in New York, Irv.

> *(IRVIN props the crate against the downstage right wall.)*

IRVIN. *(Crosses through the double doors to right of STURDYVANT.)* Okay, so they didn't sell in New York. But look at Memphis... Birmingham... Atlanta...Christ...you made a bundle.

STURDYVANT. It's not the money, Irv. You know I couldn't sleep last night? This business is bad for my nerves. My wife is after me to slow down and take a vacation. Two more years and I'm gonna get out...get into something respectable. Textiles. That's a respectable business. You know what you could do with a shipload of textiles from Ireland?

> *([Sound: A door buzzer is heard from off right.] IRVIN and STURDYVANT look at one another, relieved.)*

IRVIN. Why don't you go upstairs and let me handle it, Mel?

STURDYVANT. Remember…you're responsible for her.

> (**IRVIN** *crosses through the double doors and exits upstage the Front Hall as* **STURDYVANT** *climbs the spiral staircase, goes into the Control Booth and closes the door behind him.*)

IRVIN. *(From off right.)* How you boys doing, Cutler? Come on in.

> (**TOLEDO** *enters down the Front Hall, carrying a book and a newspaper, goes through the double doors and holds the upstage side of the double doors open as* **CUTLER** *enters, carrying a trombone case and a guitar case, followed by* **SLOW DRAG**, *struggling with a string bass in a soft case.* **CUTLER** *crosses to above the folding chairs and puts the cases on the floor.* **SLOW DRAG** *lays down his bass right of the cane chair.* **IRVIN** *enters down the Front Hall and crosses into the Studio.*)

Where's Ma? Is she with you?

CUTLER. I don't know, Mr. Irvin. She told us to be here at one o'clock. That's all I know.

> (**TOLEDO** *releases the upstage door, crosses to the piano, takes off his gloves and stuffs them into his coat pocket.*)

IRVIN. Where's…uh…the horn player…is he coming with Ma?

CUTLER. Levee's supposed to be here same as we is. I reckon he'll be here in a minute. I can't rightly say.

IRVIN. Well, come on… I'll show you to the bandroom, let you get set up and rehearsed. (**IRVIN** *crosses to the left door and flips the light switch above the piano. [Lights: The Back Hall lamps come on, illuminating the Back Hall.]* **IRVIN** *crosses to left of* **CUTLER** *as* **SLOW DRAG** *picks up his bass.*) You boys hungry? I'll call over to the deli and get some sandwiches. Get you fed and ready to make some music.

(TOLEDO exits through the left door followed by SLOW DRAG. CUTLER picks up a case in each hand and starts to follow. IRVIN takes a piece of paper from his vest pocket and holds it up. Loudly:)

Cutler...here's the list of songs we're gonna record. *(IRVIN glances up at the control booth, tucks the paper into one of CUTLER'S full hands and CUTLER exits through the left door. IRVIN starts to follow.)*

STURDYVANT. *(Over the speaker.)* Irvin...what's happening? Where's Ma?

IRVIN. *(Turns back into the studio.)* Everything's under control, Mel. I got it under control.

STURDYVANT. *(Grows more animated.)* Where's Ma? How come she isn't with the band?

IRVIN. She'll be here in a minute, Mel. Let me get these boys down to the bandroom, huh?

(IRVIN exits through the left door. TOLEDO opens the bandroom door and enters, followed by SLOW DRAG. TOLEDO crosses to the piano and drops the book and newspaper on top of it. SLOW DRAG carries his bass to behind the piano and lays it down on its side. CUTLER enters the bandroom as IRVIN appears in the doorway and flips the light switch right of the door. [Lights: The overhead bandroom lights come on, illuminating the bandroom. The studio slowly dims.])

IRVIN. You boys go ahead and rehearse. I'll let you know when Ma comes.

(IRVIN crosses into the back hall and closes the bandroom door. CUTLER leans his guitar case against the wall left of the lockers and crosses to the downstage right bench. He puts the trombone case under the bench as TOLEDO takes off his hat and coat, drops them on the downstage end of the piano and sits on the piano chair. SLOW DRAG crosses to the upstage center bench and sits.)

CUTLER. *(Crosses to* TOLEDO *and holds out the piece of paper.)* What we got here, Toledo?

> (IRVIN *appears in the left doorway and crosses into the closet. [Lights: The closet light goes out.])*

TOLEDO. *(Takes the paper and reads it.)* We got… "Prove It On Me" … "Hear Me Talking to You" … "Ma Rainey's Black Bottom" …and "Moonshine Blues."

> (IRVIN *enters the studio, closes the left door and crosses to the double doors.* STURDYVANT *looks down from the control booth as* IRVIN *opens the upstage side of the double doors and exits upstage the front hall.* STURDYVANT *leaves the control booth, climbs down the spiral staircase and follows* IRVIN *upstage the front hall.)*

CUTLER. *(Takes the paper, crosses to the Bandroom door and opens the door.)* Where Mr. Irvin go? Them ain't the songs Ma told me. *(Steps into the back hall and looks up the stairway.)*

SLOW DRAG. *(Crosses to the upstage center bench and sits.)* I wouldn't worry about it if I were you, Cutler. They'll get it straightened out. Ma will get it straightened out.

CUTLER. *(Turns to* SLOW DRAG.*)* I just don't want no trouble about these songs, that's all. Ma ain't told me them songs. She told me something else. *(*CUTLER *steps back into the bandroom, closes the door, and crosses to upstage left of the piano.)*

SLOW DRAG. What she tell you?

CUTLER. This Moonshine Blues wasn't in it. That's one of Bessie's songs.

TOLEDO. Slow Drag's right… I wouldn't worry about it. Let them straighten it up.

CUTLER. Levee know what time he's supposed to be here?

SLOW DRAG. Levee gone out to spend your four dollars. He left the hotel this morning talking about he was gonna go buy some shoes. Say it's the first time he ever beat you shooting craps.

CUTLER. *(Turns to the lockers and opens the left locker, takes off his coat, hangs it in the locker, and closes it.)* Do he know what time he's supposed to be here? That's what I wanna know. I ain't thinking about no four dollars.

SLOW DRAG. Levee sure was thinking about it. That four dollars like to burn a hole in his pocket.

CUTLER. *(Crosses to right of* **SLOW DRAG.***)* Well, he's supposed to be here at one o'clock. That's what time Ma said. That nigger get out in the streets with that four dollars and ain't no telling when he's liable to show. *(Crosses to right of* **TOLEDO,** *as* **SLOW DRAG** *rises, crosses right around the bench, takes off his hat and coat and hangs them in the open locker.)* You ought to have seen him at the club last night, Toledo. Trying to talk to some gal Ma had with her.

TOLEDO. You ain't got to tell me. I know how Levee do.

([Sound: The door buzzer is heard from off right.])

SLOW DRAG. *(Reaches into the locker and takes a half-pint bottle of bourbon from his coat pocket.)* Levee tried to talk to that gal and got his feelings hurt. She didn't want no part of him. She told Levee he'd have to turn his money green before he could talk with her.

> **(IRVIN** *enters down the front hall, followed by* **LEVEE,** *carrying a horn case and a shoe box.* **IRVIN** *holds open the downstage side of the double doors and points at the left door.* **LEVEE** *enters the Studio, crosses to the left door, opens it and exits into the Back Hall, closing the door.* **IRVIN** *exits upstage the Front Hall; the double door swings shut.)*

CUTLER. She out for what she can get. Anybody could see that.

SLOW DRAG. That's why Levee run out to buy some shoes. He's looking to make an impression on that gal. *(Opens the bottle and takes a drink.)*

CUTLER. *(Crosses to the downstage right chair, sits and lifts the trombone case onto the bench.)* What the hell she gonna do with his shoes? She can't do nothing with the nigger's shoes.

TOLEDO. Let me hit that, Slow Drag.

SLOW DRAG. *(Hands the bottle to* **TOLEDO.***)* This some of that good Chicago bourbon!

> *(***LEVEE*** *opens the bandroom door, abruptly and slams it shut behind him. He crosses to the piano and drops the horn case on top of it.)*

CUTLER. Levee...where Mr. Irvin go?

LEVEE. Hell, I ain't none of his keeper. He gone on down the hall.

SLOW DRAG. What you got there, Levee?

LEVEE. *(Takes a pair of shiney new shoes from the shoe box and holds them up; mockingly:)* Look here, Cutler... I got me some shoes!

CUTLER. Nigger, I ain't studying you.

> *(***LEVEE*** *crosses right to above the upstage center bench, drops the empty shoebox on top of the lockers, then crosses to below the bench and sits.)*

TOLEDO. How much you pay for something like that, Levee?

LEVEE. *(Taking off his old shoes.)* Eleven dollars. Four dollars of it belong to Cutler. *(Putting on his new shoes.)*

SLOW DRAG. Levee say if it wasn't for Cutler...he would have no new shoes!

CUTLER. I ain't thinking about Levee or his shoes. Come on...let's get ready to rehearse.

SLOW DRAG. *(Crosses to behind the piano, picks up the bass and begins to remove the casing.)* I'm with you on that score, Cutler. I wanna get out of here. I don't want to be around here all night. When it comes time to go up there and record them songs... I just wanna go up there and do it. Last time it took us all day and half the night.

TOLEDO. Ain't but four songs on the list. Last time we recorded six songs.

SLOW DRAG. It felt like it was sixteen!

LEVEE. *(Rises and struts around, admiring the new shoes.)* Yeah! Now I'm ready! I can play me some good music now! *(Glances up from the shoes, stops and looks around the room.)* Damn! They done changed things around. Don't never leave well enough alone. *(He picks up the old shoes, crosses right around the bench and puts the old shoes in the shoebox on the lockers.* **CUTLER** *opens the trombone case.)*

TOLEDO. Everything changing all the time. Even the air you breathing change. You got monoxide, hydrogen... changing all the time. Skin changing...different molecules and everything.

LEVEE. *(Opens the third locker from the left, takes off his coat and scarf, hangs them in the locker and closes it.)* Nigger, what is you talking about? I'm talking about the room. I ain't talking about no skin and air. I'm talking about something I can see! Last time the bandroom was upstairs. This time it's downstairs. Next time it be over there. I'm talking about what I can see. I ain't talking about no molecules or nothing.

> *(***CUTLER*** *begins to assemble his trombone.)*

TOLEDO. Hell, I know what you talking about. I just said everything changing. I know what you talking about, but you don't know what I'm talking about.

LEVEE. *(Crosses right around the bench and faces* **TOLEDO***; points at the bandroom door.)* That door! Nigger, you see that door? That's what I'm talking about. That door wasn't there before.

> *(***SLOW DRAG*** *drops the bass case in the upstage left corner and carries the bass to upstage right of the piano.)*

CUTLER. Levee, you wouldn't know your right from your left. This is where they used to keep the recording horns and things...and damn if that door wasn't there.

How in hell else you gonna get in here? Now if you talking about they done switched rooms, you right. But don't go telling me that damn door wasn't there!

SLOW DRAG. *(Takes* **LEVEE**'s *horn case off the piano and drops it on the upstage center bench with a bang.)* Damn the door and let's get set up. I wanna get out of here.

LEVEE. Toledo started all that about the door. I'm just saying that things change.

TOLEDO. What the hell you think I was saying? Things change. The air and everything. Now you gonna say you was saying it. You gonna fit two propositions on the same track...run them into each other, and because they crash you gonna say it's the same train.

LEVEE. Now this nigger talking about trains! We done went from the air to the skin to the door...and now trains. *(Crosses toward* **TOLEDO**.*)* Toledo, I'd like to be inside your head for five minutes. Just to see how you think. You done got more shit piled up and mixed up in there than the devil got sinners. You been reading too many goddamn books. *(Crosses to the upstage right corner and looks at himself in the mirror.)*

TOLEDO. What you care about how much I read? I'm gonna ignore you 'cause you ignorant.

SLOW DRAG. Come on, let's rehearse the music.

LEVEE. You ain't got to rehearse that...ain't nothing but old jug band music. *(Steps up onto the crates and admires his shoes in the mirror.)* They need one of them jug bands for this.

SLOW DRAG. Don't make me no difference. Long as we get paid.

LEVEE. That ain't what I'm talking about, nigger. I'm talking about art!

SLOW DRAG. What's drawing got to do with it?

LEVEE. *(Points at* **SLOW DRAG**.*)* Where you get this nigger from, Cutler? He sound like one of them Alabama niggers.

CUTLER. Slow Drag's alright. It's you talking all the weird shit about art. Just play the piece, nigger. You wanna be one of them...what you call...virtuoso or something, you in the wrong place. You ain't no Buddy Bolden or King Oliver...you just an old trumpet player come a dime a dozen. Talking about art.

LEVEE. *(Jumps down from the crates, crosses to the upstage center bench and sits.)* What is you? I don't see your name in lights.

CUTLER. I just plays the piece. Whatever they want. I don't go talking about art and criticizing other people's music.

LEVEE. *(Moves his horn case to the right end of the bench, opens it and takes out a silver-plated cornet.)* I ain't like you, Cutler. I got talent! Me and this horn...we's tight! If my daddy knowed I was gonna turn out like this he would've named me Gabriel.

> *(SLOW DRAG smiles derisively at LEVEE and plucks a single low note on his bass.)*

I'm gonna get me a band and make me some records. I done give Mr. Sturdyvant some of my songs I wrote and he say he's gonna let me record them when I get my band together. *(LEVEE replaces the horn in the case, takes out some sheet music and waves it at CUTLER.)* I just gotta finish the last part of this song. Mr. Sturdyvant want me to write another part to this song.

SLOW DRAG. *(Looks over LEVEE's shoulder at the sheet music.)* How you learn to write music, Levee?

LEVEE. I just picked it up...like you pick up anything. Miss Eula used to play the piano...she learned me a lot. I knows how to play real music...not this old jug band shit. *(Crosses his legs; conceitedly:)* I got style!

TOLEDO. Everybody got style.

> *(SLOW DRAG crosses to upstage right of the piano.)*

Style ain't nothing but keeping the same idea from beginning to end. Everybody got it.

LEVEE. But everybody can't play like I do. Everybody can't have their own band.

CUTLER. Well, until you get your own band where you can play what you want, you just play the piece and stop complaining. I told you when you came on here, this ain't none of them hot bands. This is an accompaniment band. You play Ma's music when you here. *(Takes a rag from the trombone case and polishes the trombone.)*

LEVEE. *(Drops the sheet music into the cornet case.)* I got sense enough to know that. Hell, I can look at you all and see what kind of band it is. I can look at Toledo and see what kind of band it is.

TOLEDO. Toledo ain't said nothing to you now. Don't let Toledo get started. You can't even spell music, much less play it.

LEVEE. What you talking about? I can spell music. *(Leaps up, pulls out a roll of bills and peels off a single dollar bill.)* I got a dollar say I can spell it! Put your dollar up. Where your dollar? (LEVEE *slaps the dollar bill on the floor downstage left of* TOLEDO.) Now, come on. Put your dollar up. Talking about I can't spell music.

TOLEDO. Alright, I'm gonna show you. *(Slowly rises, pulls a dollar bill from his pocket and places it on top of* LEVEE's *bill.)* Cutler. Slow Drag. You hear this? The nigger betting me a dollar he can spell music. I don't want no shit now! (TOLEDO *sits. Confidently:)* Alright. Go ahead. Spell it.

LEVEE. It's a bet then. Talking about I can't spell music.

TOLEDO. Go ahead then. Spell it. Music. Spell it.

LEVEE. I can spell it, nigger! M-U-S-I-K. There! *(Leaps toward the dollar bills.)*

TOLEDO. *(Steps on the bills and blocks* LEVEE *with his arm.)* Naw! Naw! Leave that money alone! You ain't spelled it.

LEVEE. What you mean I ain't spelled it? I said M-U-S-I-K!

TOLEDO. That ain't how you spell it! That ain't how you spell it! It's M-U-S-I-C! C, nigger! Not K! C! M-U-S-I-C! *(Scoops up the bills and slips the money into his coat pocket.)*

LEVEE. What you mean, C? Who say it's C?

TOLEDO. Cutler! Slow Drag. Tell this fool.

> (**TOLEDO** *picks up his newspaper and begins to read.* **CUTLER** *and* **SLOW DRAG** *look away sheepishly and play a few notes on their instruments.* **LEVEE** *looks at* **TOLEDO,** *expectantly.* **TOLEDO** *looks at* **LEVEE,** *then at* **SLOW DRAG** *and* **CUTLER.**)

Well, I'll be a monkey's uncle! *(Drops the newspaper on the piano, pulls the dollars out of his pocket and hands one to* **LEVEE.**) Here's your dollar back, Levee. I done won it, you understand. I done won the dollar. But if don't nobody know but me, how am I gonna prove it to you?

LEVEE. *(Stuffs the bill into his pants pocket.)* You just mad 'cause I spelled it.

TOLEDO. Spelled what! M-U-S-I-K don't spell nothing. I just wish there was some way I could show you the right and wrong of it. How you gonna know something if the other fellow done know if you're right or not? Now I can't even be sure that I'm spelling it right. *(Picks up the newspaper.)*

LEVEE. That's what I'm talking about. You don't know it. Talking about C. You ought to give me that dollar I won from you. *(**LEVEE** sits on the upstage center bench.)*

TOLEDO. Alright. Alright. *(Drops his newspaper on the piano and turns toward* **LEVEE.**) I'm gonna show you how ridiculous you sound. You know the Lord's Prayer?

LEVEE. *(Slides down the bench toward* **TOLEDO;** *eagerly:)* Why? You wanna bet a dollar on that?

TOLEDO. Just answer the question. Do you know the Lord's Prayer or don't you?

LEVEE. Yeah, I know it. What of it?

TOLEDO. Cutler?

CUTLER. What you Cutlering me for? I ain't got nothing to do with it. *(Leans the trombone against the bench and takes a tobacco pouch and a package of cigarette papers from* *the trombone case, then closes the case and puts it under the bench.)*

TOLEDO. I just want to show the man how ridiculous he is.

CUTLER. Both of you all sound like damn fools. Arguing about something silly. Yeah, I know the Lord's Prayer. My daddy was a deacon in the church. Come asking me if I know the Lord's Prayer. Yeah, I know it.

TOLEDO. Slow Drag?

SLOW DRAG. *(Uncertainly.)* Yeah.

TOLEDO. Alright. Now I'm gonna tell you a story to show just how ridiculous he sound. There was these two fellows, see. So, the one of them go up to this church and commence to taking up the church learning. The other fellow see him out on the road and he say... I done heard you talking up the church learning. Say... is you learning anything up there? The other one say... Yeah, I done taken up the church learning and I's learning all kinds of things about the bible and what it say and all. Why you be asking? The other one say... Well, do you know the Lord's Prayer? And he say... Why sure I know the Lord's Prayer, I'm taking up learning at the church ain't I? I know the Lord's Prayer backwards and forwards. And the other fellow say... I bet you five dollars you don't know the Lord's Prayer, 'cause I don't think you knows it. I think you be going up to the church 'cause the widow Jenkins be going up there and you just wanna be sitting in the same room with her when she cross them big, fine, pretty legs she got. And the other one say... Well, I'm gonna prove you wrong and I'm gonna bet you that five dollars. So he say... Well, go on and say it then. So he commenced to saying the Lord's Prayer. He say... Now I lay me down to sleep, I pray the Lord my soul to keep... The other one say... Here's your five dollars. I didn't think you knew it.

(**TOLEDO, CUTLER** *and* **SLOW DRAG** *all laugh;* **LEVEE** *looks at them, confused.)*

Now that's just how ridiculous Levee sound. Only 'cause I knowed how to spell music, I still got my dollar.

LEVEE. That don't prove nothing. What's that supposed to prove?

TOLEDO. I'm through with it. (TOLEDO *turns away from* LEVEE *and picks up his paper, as* CUTLER *opens his tobacco pouch, takes out a rolling paper and begins to roll a cigarette.*)

SLOW DRAG. Is you all gonna rehearse this music or ain't you?

LEVEE. How many times you done played them songs? What you gotta rehearse for?

SLOW DRAG. This is a recording session. I wanna get it right the first time and get on out of here.

CUTLER. Slow Drag's right. Let's go on and rehearse and get it over with.

LEVEE. (*Picks up the sheet music, takes a pencil from his case, faces left and straddles the bench.*) You all go and rehearse then. I got to finish this song for Mr. Sturdyvant.

CUTLER. Come on, Levee... I don't want no shit now. You rehearse like everybody else. You in the band like everybody else. Mr. Sturdyvant just gonna have to wait. You got to do that on your own time. This is the band's time.

LEVEE. Well, what is you doing? You sitting there rolling a reefer talkng about let's rehearse. Toledo reading a newspaper. Hell, I'm ready if you wanna rehearse. I just say there ain't no point in it. Ma ain't here. What's the point in it?

CUTLER. Nigger, why you gotta complain all the time?

TOLEDO. Levee would complain if a gal ain't laid across his bed just right.

CUTLER. That's what I know. That's why I try to tell him just play the music and forget about it. It ain't no big thing. (*Takes a box of matches from his coat pocket and lights the cigarette.*)

TOLEDO. Levee ain't got an eye for that. He wants to tie on to some abstract component and sit down on the elemental.

(Exasperated, **SLOW DRAG** *lays down his bass behind the piano as* **CUTLER** *puts the tobacco pouch, papers and matches in his coat pocket.)*

LEVEE. This is get on Levee time, huh? Levee ain't said nothing except this some old jug band music.

TOLEDO. Under the right circumstances you'd play anything. If you know music then you play it. Straight on or off to the side. Ain't nothing abstract about it.

LEVEE. Toledo, you sound like you got a mouth full of marbles. You is the only cracker-talking nigger I know.

TOLEDO. You ought to have learned yourself to read... then you'd understand the basic understanding of everything.

SLOW DRAG. Both of you all gonna drive me crazy with that philosophy bullshit. *(Crosses above* **LEVEE** *to right of* **CUTLER.***)* Cutler, give me a reefer.

CUTLER. Ain't you got some reefer? Where's your reefer? Why you all the time asking me?

SLOW DRAG. Cutler, how long I done known you? How long we been together? Twenty-two years.

*(***CUTLER** *turns away from* **SLOW DRAG** *and continues to smoke the "reefer.")*

We been doing this together for twenty-two years. All up and down the back roads, the side roads, the front roads...we done played in the juke-joints, the whorehouses, the barn dances and city sit-downs... I done lied for you and lied with you...we done laughed together, fought together, slept in the same bed together, done sucked on the same titty...and now you don't wanna give me no reefer.

CUTLER. You see this nigger trying to talk me out of my reefer, Toledo? Running all that about how long he done knowed me and how we done sucked on the same titty. *(Turns to* **SLOW DRAG**, *laughing.)* Nigger, you still ain't getting none of my reefer!

TOLEDO. That's African.

SLOW DRAG. *(Suspiciously.)* What? What you talking about? What's African?

LEVEE. *(Defensively.)* I know he ain't talking about me. You don't see me running around in no jungle with no bone between my nose.

TOLEDO. Levee, you worse than ignorant. You ignorant without a premise. *(Turns to* **CUTLER** *and* **SLOW DRAG**.*)* Now, what I was saying is what Slow Drag was doing is African. That's what you call an African conceptualization. That's when you name the gods or call on the ancestors to achieve whatever your desires are.

SLOW DRAG. Nigger, I ain't no African! I ain't doing no African nothing!

TOLEDO. Naming all those things you and Cutler done together is like trying to solicit some reefer based on a bond of kinship. That's African. An ancestral retention. Only you forgot the name of the gods.

SLOW DRAG. I ain't forgot nothing. I was telling the nigger how cheap he is. Don't come talking that African nonsense to me.

TOLEDO. You just like Levee. No eye for taking an abstract and fixing it to a specific. There's so much that goes on around you and you can't even see it.

CUTLER. Wait a minute...wait a minute. Toledo, now when this nigger...when an African do all them things you say and name all the gods and what not...then what happens?

TOLEDO. Depends on if the gods is sympathetic with the cause for which he is calling them with the right names. Then his success comes with the right proportion of his naming. That's the way that go. *(***TOLEDO** *returns to his newspaper.)*

CUTLER. *(Hands an unlit "reefer" to* SLOW DRAG.) Here, Slow Drag. Here's a reefer. You done talked yourself up on that one.

SLOW DRAG. *(Takes the "reefer" and pulls a box of matches from his vest pocket.)* Thank you. You ought to have done that in the first place and saved me all the aggravation.

CUTLER. What I wants to know is…what the same titty we done sucked on? That's what I want to know.

SLOW DRAG. Oh, I just threw that in there to make it sound good. *(Sits on the downstage right bench and lights a match.)*

CUTLER. Nigger, you ain't right.

SLOW DRAG. I knows it. *(Lights the "reefer" and starts to take a drag.)*

CUTLER. Well, come on…let's get rehearsed. Time's wasting.

> *(He picks up the trombone, rises and plays a few notes as he crosses to the downstage left chair.* LEVEE *picks up his cornet, rises and plays.* SLOW DRAG *crosses above the upstage center bench, picks up his bass and crosses to upstage right of the piano.)*

Let's do it. "Ma Rainey's Black Bottom" A-One. A-Two. You know what to do.

> *([MUSIC:* TOLEDO *plays a short piano introduction to* "MA RAINEY'S BLACK BOTTOM" *as* LEVEE *plays a louder and faster introduction.* CUTLER *and* SLOW DRAG *join in at a leisurely tempo.* LEVEE *stops playing.])*

LEVEE. Naw! Naw! We ain't doing it that way. *([MUSIC: The Band stops playing.])* We doing my version. It say so right there on that piece of paper you got. Ask Toledo. That's what Mr. Irvin told me…say it's on the list he gave you.

CUTLER. Let me worry about what's on the list and what ain't on the list. How you gonna tell me what's on the list?

LEVEE. 'Cause I know what Mr. Irvin told me! Ask Toledo!

CUTLER. *(Irritated.)* Let me worry about what's on the list. You just play the song I say.

LEVEE. What kind of sense it make to rehearse the wrong version of the song? That's what I wanna know. Why you wanna rehearse that version?

SLOW DRAG. *(With forced patience.)* You supposed to rehearse what you gonna play. That's the way they taught me. Now, whatever version we gonna play...let's go on and rehearse it.

LEVEE. That's what I'm trying to tell the man.

CUTLER. You trying to tell me what we is and ain't gonna play. And that ain't none of your business. Your business is to play what I say.

LEVEE. *(Crowing.)* Oh, I see now. You done got jealous 'cause Mr. Irvin using my version. You done got jealous 'cause I proved I know something about music.

CUTLER. Nigger, you talk like a fool! What the hell I got to be jealous of you about? The day I get jealous of you I may as well lay down and die.

TOLEDO. Levee started all that 'cause he too lazy to rehearse. *(Turns to LEVEE.)* You ought to just go on and play the song...what difference does it make?

LEVEE. *(Steps toward CUTLER.)* Where's the paper? Look at the paper! Get the paper and look at it! See what it say. *(Turns away, disgusted.)* Gonna tell me I'm too lazy to rehearse.

CUTLER. We ain't talking about the paper. We talking about you understanding where you fit in when you around here. You just play what I say.

LEVEE. *(Turns to CUTLER; curtly:)* Look... I don't care what you play! Alright? It don't matter to me. Mr. Irvin gonna straighten it up! I don't care what you play. *(Crosses right a few steps.)*

CUTLER. Thank you. *(Turns to TOLEDO.)* Let's play this "Hear Me Talking To You" till we find out what's happening with the "Black Bottom."

(**LEVEE** and **TOLEDO** glance at one another, laugh conspiratorially and look at **SLOW DRAG**. They look at **CUTLER**. He chuckles.)

CUTLER. Slow Drag, you sing Ma's part.

(**SLOW DRAG** feigns insult then minces to center and lays his bass down on the floor.)

"Hear Me Talking To You." Let's do it. A-One. A-Two. You know what to do.

([*MUSIC:* **TOLEDO** plays a short introduction to **"HEAR ME TALKING TO YOU."** **LEVEE** and **CUTLER** join in.] **SLOW DRAG** mimes opening a bottle and drinking, then sets the imaginary bottle on the piano, picks up **TOLEDO**'s newspaper and fans himself.)

SLOW DRAG. (Singing.)
RAMBLIN' MAN MAKES NO CHANGE IN ME.
I'M GONNA RAMBLE BACK TO MY USED-TO-BE, AH –
HEAR ME TALKING TO YOU, I DON'T BITE MY TONGUE.
YOU WANT TO BE MY MAN, YOU GOT TO FETCH IT WITH
    YOU WHEN YOU COME.

EVE AND ADAM IN THE GARDEN TAKING A CHANCE.
ADAM DIDN'T TAKE TIME TO GET HIS PANTS, AH –
HEAR ME TALKING TO YOU, I DON'T BITE MY TONGUE.
YOU WANT TO BE MY MAN, YOU GOT TO FETCH IT WITH
    YOU WHEN YOU COME.

(**IRVIN** enters down the front hall, crosses through the double doors and into the studio. He crosses left and exits through the left door into the back hall.)

OUR OLD CAT SWALLOWED A BALL OF YARN.
WHEN THE KITTENS WAS BORN THEY HAD SWEATERS ON.

(**IRVIN** opens the bandroom door, crosses to behind the piano, leans on it and listens.)

HEAR ME TALKING TO YOU, I DON'T BITE MY TONGUE.
YOU WANT TO BE MY MAN, YOU GOT TO FETCH IT WITH
    YOU WHEN YOU COME.

(**SLOW DRAG** *turns toward the piano, sees* **IRVIN**
*and stops. [**MUSIC:** The band stops.] All laugh.*
SLOW DRAG *returns the newspaper to the piano
and crosses to the bass.*)

IRVIN. *(Seriously.)* Any of you boys know what's keeping Ma?

CUTLER. Can't say Mr. Irvin. She'll be along directly, I
reckon. I talked to her this morning, she say she'll be
here in time to rehearse.

IRVIN. Well, you boys go ahead. *(Starts toward the bandroom
door.)*

CUTLER. Mr. Irvin, about these songs... Levee say...

IRVIN. *(Turns to* **CUTLER.**) Whatever's on the list, Cutler.
You got that list I gave you?

CUTLER. *(Pats his coat pocket.)* Yessir, I got it right here.

IRVIN. Whatever's on there. Whatever that says. *(Turns
toward the bandroom door again.)*

CUTLER. I'm asking about this "Black Bottom" piece...
Levee say...

IRVIN. *(Crosses to right of* **CUTLER.**) Oh, it's on the list. "Ma
Rainey's Black Bottom" is on the list.

CUTLER. I know it's on the list. I wanna know what version.
We got two versions of that song.

IRVIN. Oh. Levee's arrangement. *(Turns to* **LEVEE;** *he grins.)*
We're using Levee's arrangement.

CUTLER. OK. I got that straight. Now, this "Moonshine
Blues" ...

IRVIN. We'll work it out with Ma, Cutler. Just rehearse
whatever's on the list and use Levee's arrangement on
that "Black Bottom" piece. *(He exits through the bandroom
door and closes it.* **SLOW DRAG** *picks up the bass and crosses
to upstage right of the piano.)*

LEVEE. *(Crosses toward* **CUTLER** *a step; triumphantly:)* See, I
told you! It don't mean nothing when I say it. You got
to wait for Mr. Irvin to say it. Well, I told you the way it
is.

CUTLER. Levee, the sooner you understand it ain't what you say, or what Mr. Irvin say...it's what Ma say that counts.

SLOW DRAG. Don't nobody say when it comes to Ma. She's gonna do what she wants to do. Ma says what happens to her.

LEVEE. Hell, the man's the one putting out the record! He's gonna put out what he wanna put out!

SLOW DRAG. *(Crosses to left of* **LEVEE.***)* He's gonna put out what Ma want him to put out.

LEVEE. *(Raises his hand, threateningly, toward* **SLOW DRAG.***)* You heard what the man told you... "Ma Rainey's Black Bottom," Levee's arrangement. There you go! *(Pokes* **SLOW DRAG** *on the nose.)* That's what he told you.

SLOW DRAG. *(Crosses to upstage right of the piano.)* What you gonna do, Cutler?

CUTLER. Ma ain't told me what version. Let's go on and play it Levee's way.

TOLEDO. *(Pedantically.)* See, now... I'll tell you something. As long as the colored man look to white folks to put the crown on what he say...as long as he looks to white folks for approval...then he ain't never gonna find out who he is and what he's about. He's just gonna be about what white folks want him to be about. That's one sure thing.

LEVEE. I'm just trying to show Cutler where he's wrong.

CUTLER. Cutler don't need you to show him nothing.

SLOW DRAG. Come on, let's get this shit rehearsed! You all can bicker afterward!

CUTLER. Levee's confused about who the boss is. He don't know Ma's the boss.

LEVEE. Ma's the boss on the road! We at a recording session. Mr. Sturdyvant and Mr. Irvin say what's gonna be here! We's in Chicago, we ain't in Memphis. I don't know why you all wanna pick me about it, shit! I'm with Slow Drag...let's go on and get it rehearsed.

CUTLER. Alright. Alright. I know how to solve this. "Ma Rainey's Black Bottom," Levee's version. Let's do it. Come on. A-One. A-Two...

TOLEDO. How that first part go again, Levee?

LEVEE. It go like this.

> ([*MUSIC:* LEVEE *plays a short staccato introduction to his version of the* "BLACK BOTTOM."])

That's to get the people's attention to the song. That's when you and Slow Drag come in with the rhythm part. Me and Cutler play on the breaks. (*Paces in circles; animatedly:*) Now we gonna dance it...but we ain't gonna countrify it. This ain't no barn dance. This a city dance. We gonna play it like...

CUTLER. (*Impatiently.*) The man asked you how the first part go. He don't wanna hear all that. Just tell him how the piece go.

TOLEDO. I got it. I got it. Let's go. I know how to do it.

CUTLER. Ma Rainey's Black Bottom. Levee's Version. One. Two. You know what to do.

> ([*MUSIC:* LEVEE *plays his introduction to the* "BLACK BOTTOM"; *then the band joins in at a slower tempo.* LEVEE *stops playing.*] *He glares at the band, infuriated.*)

LEVEE. You all got to keep up now. You playing in the wrong time.

> ([*MUSIC:* *The band stops playing.*])

Ma come in over the top. She got to find her own way in.

CUTLER. Nigger, will you let us play this song. When you get your own band...then you tell them that nonsense. We know how to play the piece. I was playing music before you was born. Gonna tell me how to play.

> (SLOW DRAG *examines the strings of the bass.*)

Alright. Let's try it again. A-One. A-Two...

SLOW DRAG. Cutler, wait till I fix this. This string started to unravel. *(Carries his bass downstage right and faces* **CUTLER.***)* And you know I want to play Levee's music right.

LEVEE. *(Crosses to behind* **SLOW DRAG.***)* If you was any kind of a musician you'd take care of your instrument. Keep it in tip top order. If you was any kind of a musician... I'd let you be in my band.

SLOW DRAG. Shhheeeeet! *(Turns upstage right and inadvertently steps on* **LEVEE***'s shoe.)*

LEVEE. Damn, Slow Drag! Watch them big-ass shoes you got.

SLOW DRAG. *(Crosses to upstage right and sits on the crates, facing downstage, holding his bass.)* Boy, ain't nobody done nothing to you.

LEVEE. *(Crosses to the upstage center bench, takes a rag out of his horn case and wipes his shoe.)* You done stepped on my shoes.

SLOW DRAG. Move them the hell out the way then. You was in my way... I wasn't in your way. *(Stretches one foot out toward* **LEVEE***; mockingly:)* You can shine these when you get done, Levee. *(All laugh except* **LEVEE.***)*

CUTLER. *(Leans his trombone against the piano, takes another "reefer" and a box of matches out of his pocket and lights the "reefer.")* If I had them shoes Levee got, I could buy me a whole suit of clothes.

LEVEE. *(Tosses the rag back into the horn case and sits on the upstage center bench.)* What kind of difference it make what kind of shoes I got? Ain't nothing wrong with having nice shoes. I ain't said nothing about your shoes. Why you wanna talk about me and my Florsheims?

CUTLER. *(Puts the matchbox in his pocket.)* Any man...who takes a whole week's pay...and puts it on some shoes— you understand what I mean, what you walk around on the ground with—is a fool! And I don't mind telling him.

LEVEE. What difference it make to you, Cutler!

Good times is what makes life worth living. Now, you take the white man...the white man don't know how to have a good time. That's why he's troubled all the time. He don't know how to have a good time. He don't know how to laugh at life.

LEVEE. *(Crosses to left of* SLOW DRAG.*)* That's what the problem is with Toledo...reading all them books and things. He done got to the point where he forgot how to laugh and have a good time. Just like the white man.

TOLEDO. I know how to have a good time as well as the next man. I said, there's got to be more to life than having a good time. I said the colored man ought to be doing more than just trying to have a good time all the time.

LEVEE. Well, what is you doing, nigger? Talking all them high-falutin ideas about making a better world for the colored man. What is you doing to make it better? You playing the music and looking for your next piece of pussy same as we is. What is you doing? That's what I wanna know. Tell him, Cutler.

CUTLER. You all leave Cutler out of this. Cutler ain't got nothing to do with it.

TOLEDO. Levee, you just about the most ignorant nigger I know. Sometimes I wonder why I even bother to try and talk with you.

LEVEE. Well, what is you doing? Talking that shit to me about I'm ignorant! What is you doing! You just a whole lot of mouth. A great big windbag. Thinking you smarter than everybody else. What is you doing, huh?

TOLEDO. It ain't just me, fool! It's everybody! What you think... I'm gonna solve the colored man's problems by myself? I said, we. You understand that? We. That's every living colored man in the world got to do his share. Got to do his part. I ain't talking about what I'm gonna do...or what you or Cutler or Slow Drag or anybody else. I'm talking about all of us together. What all of us is gonna do. That's what I'm talking about, nigger. *(Turns away from* **LEVEE** *and picks up his newspaper.)*

LEVEE. *(Looks at* **TOLEDO** *for a moment, then crosses to* **TOLEDO** *and puts a hand on his shoulder, subdued.)* Well, why didn't you say that then?

> *(***TOLEDO** *shakes off* **LEVEE**'*s hand.* **LEVEE** *crosses to below the upstage center bench.)*

CUTLER. Toledo, I don't know why you waste your time on this fool.

TOLEDO. That's what I'm trying to figure out.

LEVEE. Now there go Cutler with his shit. Calling me a fool. You wasn't even in the conversation. Now you gonna take sides and call me a fool.

CUTLER. Hell, I was listening to the man. I got sense enough to know what he saying. I could tell it straight back to you.

LEVEE. Well, you go on with it. But I'll tell you this… I ain't gonna be too many more of your fools. I'll tell you that. Now you can put that in your pipe and smoke it.

CUTLER. Boy, ain't nobody studying you. Telling me what to put in my pipe. Who's you to tell me what to do?

LEVEE. *(Crosses toward the crates.)* Alright, I ain't nobody. Don't pay me no mind. I ain't nobody.

TOLEDO. Levee, you ain't nothing but the devil.

LEVEE. There you go! That's who I am. I'm the devil. I ain't nothing but the devil.

CUTLER. I can see that. That's something you know about. You know all about the devil.

LEVEE. *(Crosses toward* **CUTLER**.*)* I ain't saying what I know. I know plenty. What you know about the devil? Telling me what I know. What you know?

SLOW DRAG. I know a man sold his soul to the devil.

LEVEE. *(Crosses to the upstage center bench and sits, facing* **SLOW DRAG**.*)* There you go! That's the only thing I ask about the devil…to see him coming so I can sell his this one I got. 'Cause if there's a God up there…he done went to sleep. (*Takes his cornet and a rag from the case and polishes the cornet.*)

SLOW DRAG. Sold his soul to the devil himself. Name of Eliza Cotter. Lived in Tuscaloosa County, Alabama. The devil came by and he done upped and sold him his soul.

CUTLER. How you know the man done sold his soul to the devil, nigger? You talking that old woman foolishness.

SLOW DRAG. Everybody know. It wasn't no secret. He went around working for the devil and everybody knowed it. Carried him a bag...one of them carpet bags. Folks say he carried the devil's papers and what not where he put your fingerprint on the paper with blood.

LEVEE. Where he at now? That's what I want to know. He can put my whole handprint if he want to!

CUTLER. That's the damnedest thing I ever heard! Folks kill me with that talk.

TOLEDO. (*Puts the newspaper on the piano and turns to* CUTLER.) Oh, that's real enough, alright. Some folks go arm in arm with the devil, shoulder to shoulder and talk to him all the time. That's real, ain't nothing wrong in believing that.

SLOW DRAG. That's what I'm saying. Eliza Cotter is one of them. Alright. The man living up there in an old shack on Ben Foster's place, shoeing mules and horses, making them charms and things in secret. He hooked up with the devil. Showed one day all fancied out with just the finest clothes you ever seen on a colored man... dressed just like one of them crackers...and carrying this bag with them papers and things in. Alright. Had a pocketful of money, just living the life of a rich man. Ain't done no more work or nothing. Just had him a string of women he run around with and throw his money away on. Bought him a big fine house...well, it wasn't that big, but it did have one of them white picket fences around it. Used to hire a man once a week just to paint that fence. Messed around there and one of the fellows of them gals he was messing with got fixed on him wrong and Eliza killed him. And he laughed about it. Sheriff come and arrest him, and then let him go. And he went around in that town laughing about killing this fellow. Trial come up, and the judge cut him loose. He must have been in converse with the devil, too... 'cause he cut him loose and give him a bottle of whiskey! Folks ask what done happened to make him change, and he'd tell them straight out he done sold his soul to the devil and asked them if they wanted to sell theirs 'cause he could arrange it for them. Preacher see him coming, used to cross on the other side of the road. He'd just stand there and laugh at the preacher and call him a fool to his face.

CUTLER. Well, whatever happened to this fellow? What come of him? A man who, as you say, done sold his soul to the devil is bound to come to a bad end.

TOLEDO. I don't know about that. The devil's strong. The devil ain't no pushover.

SLOW DRAG. Oh, the devil had him under his wing alright. Took good care of him. He ain't wanted for nothing.

CUTLER. What happened to him? That's what I want to know.

SLOW DRAG. Last I heard, he headed up north with that bag of his handing out hundred dollar bills on the spot to whoever wanted to sign on with the devil. That's what I hear tell of him.

CUTLER. That's a bunch of fool talk. I don't know how you fix your mouth to tell that story. I don't believe you.

SLOW DRAG. I ain't asking you to believe it. I'm just telling you the facts of it.

LEVEE. I sure wish I knew where he went. He wouldn't have to convince me long. Hell, I'd even help him sign people up.

CUTLER. Nigger, God's gonna strike you down with that blasphemy you talking.

LEVEE. Oh, shit! God don't mean nothing to me. Let him strike me! *(Stands and looks upward; mockingly:)* Here I am standing right here. What you talking about he's gonna strike me? Here I am! Let him strike me! I ain't scared of him. *(Looks at **CUTLER**, disdainfully.)* Talking that stuff to me.

CUTLER. Alright. You gonna be sorry. You gonna fix yourself to have bad luck. Ain't nothing gonna work for you.

([Sound: The door buzzer is heard from off right.])

LEVEE. Bad luck? What I care about bad luck? You talking simple. I ain't had nothing but bad luck all my life. Couldn't get no worse. What the hell I care about some bad luck? Hell, I eat it everyday for breakfast! You dumber than I thought you was…talking about bad luck. *(Turns away from **CUTLER** and sits on the upstage center bench.)*

CUTLER. Alright, nigger, you'll see! Can't tell a fool nothing. You'll see.

IRVIN. *(Enters down the front hall, crosses through the double doors into the studio, then crosses to the left door, opens it and shouts down the back hall.)* Cutler…you boys' sandwiches are up here… Cutler?

CUTLER. Yessir, Mr. Irvin…be right there. *(Starts to rise.)*

TOLEDO. *(Rises and crosses to the bandroom door.)* I'll walk up there and get them.

*(He crosses into the back hall and closes the door. Simultaneously, **IRVIN** crosses back into the Studio, closes the left door and moves to below the piano as **STURDYVANT** enters down the front hall, comes through the double doors into the studio and crosses to right of **IRVIN**.)*

STURDYVANT. *(Anxiously.)* Irv…what's happening? Is she here yet? Was that her?

IRVIN. It's the sandwiches, Mel. I told you… I'll let you know when she comes, huh?

(TOLEDO opens the left door a few inches, glances at STURDYVANT and quietly backs into the back hall, closing the door behind him.)

STURDYVANT. What's keeping her? Do you know what time it is? Have you looked at the clock? You told me she'd be here. You told me you'd take care of it.

IRVIN. *(Crosses to the right folding chair and sits; exasperated:)* Mel, for Chrissakes! What do you want from me? What do you want me to do?

STURDYVANT. *(Points at the clock above the piano.)* Look what time it is, Irv. You told me she'd be here.

IRVIN. She'll be here, okay? I don't know what's keeping her. You know they're always late, Mel.

STURDYVANT. You should have went by the hotel and made sure she was on time. You should have taken care of this. That's what you told me, huh? "I'll take care of it."

IRVIN. Okay! So I didn't go by the hotel! What do you want me to do? She'll be here, okay? The band's here… she'll be here.

(TOLEDO quietly opens the left door and steps into the studio.)

STURDYVANT. Okay, Irv. I'll take your word. But if she doesn't come… *(Turns upstage right and crosses to the spiral staircase.)* …if she doesn't come… *(He climbs the staircase, goes into the control booth, and closes the door. TOLEDO steps toward IRVIN, hesitantly.)*

TOLEDO. Mr. Irvin… I come up for the sandwiches.

IRVIN. *(Rises and crosses to right of TOLEDO.)* Say…uh… look…one o'clock, right? She said one o'clock.

TOLEDO. That's what time she told us. Say be here at one o'clock.

IRVIN. Do you know what's keeping her? Do you know why she ain't here?

TOLEDO. I can't say Mr. Irvin. Told us one o'clock.

([Sound: The door buzzer begins to ring incessantly off right.] IRVIN goes quickly through the double

> doors and exits upstage the front hall. [Sound: The
> door buzzer stops ringing.] Shouting and scuffling
> is heard off right.)

MA RAINEY. (Enters down the front hall, rushes furiously through
the double doors and crosses to above the platform, followed
by IRVIN, DUSSIE MAE carrying a small purse, SYLVESTER
carrying a large loop-handled bag, and a POLICEMAN
carrying a nightstick.) Irvin...you better tell this man
who I am!

> (IRVIN crosses to below the cane chair, DUSSIE MAE
> crosses to upstage left of MA, SYLVESTER crosses to
> right of DUSSIE MAE and the POLICEMAN crosses
> to left of the radiator.)

You better get him straight!

IRVIN. Ma, do you know what time it is? Do you have any
idea? We've been waiting...

DUSSIE MAE. (To SYLVESTER.) If you was watching where you
was going...

SYLVESTER. I was watching...what you mean?

IRVIN. (Turns away and notices the POLICEMAN for the first
time.) What's going on here? Officer...what's the
matter?

MA RAINEY. Tell the man who he's messing with!

POLICEMAN. Do you know this lady?

MA RAINEY. Just tell the man who I am. That's all you got
to do!

POLICEMAN. (Angrily.) Lady will you let me talk, huh?

MA RAINEY. Tell the man who I am!

IRVIN. (Turns to MA.) Wait a minute...wait a minute! Let me
handle it. Ma, will you let me handle it?

MA RAINEY. Tell him who he's messing with!

IRVIN. Okay! Okay! Just give me a chance! (Turns to the
POLICEMAN.) Officer...this is one of our recording
artists... Ma Rainey.

MA RAINEY. Madame Rainey! Get it straight! Madame Rainey! Talking about taking me to jail.

IRVIN. *(Steps toward* MA.*)* Look, Ma...give me a chance, okay? Here...sit down. I'll take care of it. *(Turns back to the* POLICEMAN.*)* Officer...what's the problem?

DUSSIE MAE. It's all your fault!

SYLVESTER. I ain't done nothing...ask Ma.

POLICEMAN. Well...when I walked up on the incident...

DUSSIE MAE. *(Scornfully.)* Sylvester wrecked Ma's car.

SYLVESTER. I d-d-did not! *(To the* POLICEMAN.*)* The m-m-man ran into me!

POLICEMAN. *(To* IRVIN.*)* Look, buddy...if you want it in a nutshell...we got her charged with assault and battery.

MA RAINEY. *(Astounded.)* Assault and what for what!

DUSSIE MAE. See...we was trying to get a cab...and so Ma...

MA RAINEY. Wait a minute! I'll tell you if you want to know what happened.

> (DUSSIE MAE *crosses indignantly to left of the piano.* MA *turns to* IRVIN *and points at* SYLVESTER.*)*

Now, that's Sylvester. That's my nephew. He was driving my car...

POLICEMAN. Lady, we don't know whose car he was driving.

MA RAINEY. That's my car!

DUSSIE MAE AND SYLVESTER. *(Simultaneously.)* That's Ma's car!

MA RAINEY. What you mean you don't know whose car it is? I bought and paid for that car. Registered to me, Gertrude "Ma" Rainey!

POLICEMAN. That's what you say, lady...we still gotta check. *(To* IRVIN.*)* They hit a car on Market Street. The guy said the kid ran a stoplight.

SYLVESTER. *(Indignantly.)* What you mean? The man c-c-come around the corner and hit m-m-me!

POLICEMAN. While I was calling a paddy wagon to haul
them to the station...they try to hop into a parked cab.
The cabby said he was waiting on a fare...

MA RAINEY. The man was just sitting there. Wasn't waiting
for nobody. I don't know why he wanna tell that lie.

(DUSSIE MAE *crosses to upstage left of* MA.)

POLICEMAN. (*Wearily.*) Look, lady...will you let me tell the
story?

MA RAINEY. Go ahead and tell it then. But tell it right!

POLICEMAN. Like I say...she tries to get in this cab.
The cabbie's waiting on a fare. She starts creating a
disturbance. The cabbie gets out to try to explain the
situation to her...and she knocks him down.

DUSSIE MAE. She ain't hit him! He just fell!

SYLVESTER. He j-j-j-just slipped!

POLICEMAN. He claims she knocked him down. We got her
charged with assault and battery.

MA RAINEY. If that don't beat all to hell! I ain't touched the
man! The man was trying to reach around me to keep
his car door closed. I opened the door and it hit him
and he fell down. I ain't touched the man!

IRVIN. (*Turns to* MA; *placatingly:*) Ok. Ok... I got it straight
now, Ma. You didn't touch him. Alright? (*Takes the*
POLICEMAN *by the arm and starts toward the double doors.*)
Officer...can I see you for a moment?

DUSSIE MAE. (*To* IRVIN; *insistently:*) Ma was just trying to
open the door.

(IRVIN *stops at the double doors, annoyed.*)

SYLVESTER. He j-j-just got in t-t-the way!

MA RAINEY. Said he wasn't gonna haul no colored folks...if
you want to know the truth of it.

IRVIN. (*To* MA.) Okay, Ma... I got it straight now.

(*Turns back to the* POLICEMAN.) *Officer?*
(*He leads the* POLICEMAN *through the double
doors and into the front hall; they talk quietly.*

SYLVESTER *crosses to upstage left of the double doors and peers through the windows.* MA *crosses right around the right folding chair to* TOLEDO; DUSSIE MAE *follows to right of* MA.)

MA RAINEY. Toledo, Cutler and everybody here?

TOLEDO. Yeah, they down in the bandroom. What happened to your car?

STURDYVANT. *(Leaves the control booth and bounds down the spiral staircase.)* Irv...what's the problem? *(Stops left of* SYLVESTER *and looks around the room.)* What's going on?

(SYLVESTER *counters left as* STURDYVANT *opens the upstage side of the double doors and looks into the front hall.)*

IRVIN. *(Crosses through the open double door to right of* STURDYVANT.)* Mel, let me take care of it. I can handle it.

STURDYVANT. What's happening? What the hell's going on?

IRVIN. Let me handle it, Mel, huh?

STURDYVANT. *(Releases the double door and turns to* MA; *suspiciously:)* What's going on, Ma? What'd you do?

MA RAINEY. Sturdyvant, get on away from me! That's the last thing I need...to go through some of your shit!

IRVIN. *(Moves toward* STURDYVANT; *appeasingly:)* Mel, I'll take care of it. I'll explain it all to you. Let me handle it, huh?

(STURDYVANT *looks dubiously at* IRVIN, *then crosses to the spiral staircase, climbs up to the control booth, enters and closes the door. The* POLICEMAN *opens the upstage side of the double doors and steps into the Studio. The door swings shut.)*

POLICEMAN. *(Impatiently.)* Look, buddy, like I say...we got her charged with assault and battery...and the kid with threatening the cabbie.

SYLVESTER. (*Clutches the bag to his chest; stubbornly:*) I ain't done n-n-nothing!

MA RAINEY. You leave the boy out of it. He ain't done nothing. What's he supposed to have done?

POLICEMAN. He threatened the cabbie, lady! You just can't go around threatening people.

SYLVESTER. (*Crosses to left of* **IRVIN.**) I ain't done nothing to him! He's the one talking about he g-g-gonna get a b-b-baseball bat on me! I just told him what I'd do with it. But I ain't done nothing cause he didn't get the b-b-bat!

IRVIN. (*Takes the* **POLICEMAN** *by the arm and crosses downstage right.*) Officer...look here...

POLICEMAN. We was on our way down to the precinct...but I figured I'd do you a favor and bring her by here. I mean, if she's as important as she says she is...

IRVIN. (*Reaches into his pants pocket, pulls out a roll of bills and peels off three dollar bills.*) Look, Officer... I'm Madame Rainey's manager...it's good to meet you.

> (*He shakes the* **POLICEMAN**'s *hand and slips the dollar bills into his palm. The* **POLICEMAN** *looks at the money in his hand, then glances at* **IRVIN** *quizzically.* **IRVIN** *quickly peels off another bill and slips it into the* **POLICEMAN**'s *hand. Reassuringly:*)

As soon as we're finished with the recording session... I'll personally stop by the precinct house and straighten up this misunderstanding.

POLICEMAN. (*Looks at the money in his hand, then at* **IRVIN.**) Well... I guess that's alright. As long as someone is responsible for them. (*Puts the money in his pocket.*) No need to come down... I'll take care of it myself. (*Glares at* **MA** *and* **SYLVESTER.**) Of course, we wouldn't want nothing like this to happen again.

IRVIN. Don't worry, Officer... I'll take care of everything. Thanks for your help.

(He escorts the **POLICEMAN** *through the double doors.* **MA** *crosses to above the platform and* **DUSSIE MAE** *crosses to below the cane chair. The* **POLICEMAN** *exits upstage the front hall as* **IRVIN** *crosses back through the double doors to right of* **MA**.*)*

Here, Ma...let me take your coat. *(Takes* **MA**'*s coat and turns to* **DUSSIE MAE**; *solicitously:)* I don't believe I know you.

MA RAINEY. That's my nephew, Sylvester.

IRVIN. *(Stares at* **DUSSIE MAE**, *puzzled, then after a moment, quickly turns and crosses to* **SYLVESTER**.*)* I'm very pleased to meet you. Here...you can give me your coat. *(Takes* **SYLVESTER**'*s coat and hangs it on his arm.)*

MA RAINEY. That there is Dussie Mae.

IRVIN. *(Crosses to right of* **DUSSIE MAE**, *takes her coat and smiles broadly.)* Hello...listen Ma, just sit there and relax. The boys are in the bandroom rehearsing. You just sit and relax a minute.

MA RAINEY. *(Obstinately.)* I ain't for no sitting. I ain't never heard of such. Talking about taking me to jail. Irvin, call down there and see about my car.

IRVIN. Okay, Ma... I'll take care of it. You just relax. *(*IRVIN *crosses through the double doors and hangs the coats in the front hall peevishly.)*

MA RAINEY. Why you all keep it so cold in here?

IRVIN. *(From hall.)* Huh?

MA RAINEY. Sturdyvant try and pinch every penny he can.

*(*IRVIN *crosses back into the Studio to the radiator.)*

You all wanna make some records you better put some heat on in here or give me back my coat.

IRVIN. *(Cautiously touches the radiator.)* We got the heat turned up, Ma. It's warming up. *(Places his hand on the radiator, uncertainly.)* It'll be warm in a minute.

DUSSIE MAE. *(Whispers to* **MA**.*)* Where's the bathroom?

MA RAINEY. It's in the back, down the hall next to Sturdyvant's office. Come on, I'll show you where it is.

> *(**DUSSIE MAE** crosses to double doors and opens the upstage door.)*

Irvin, call down there and see about my car. I want my car fixed today.

IRVIN. I'll take care of everything, Ma.

> *(**MA** and **DUSSIE MAE** exit upstage the front hall; the door swings shut. **IRVIN** turns to **TOLEDO**.)*

Say...uh...uh... *(Snaps his fingers.)*

TOLEDO. Toledo.

IRVIN. Yeah, Toledo. I got the sandwiches you can take down to the rest of the boys. We'll be ready to go in a minute. *(Crosses to the double doors, followed by **TOLEDO**.)* Give you boys a chance to eat and then we'll be ready to go.

> *(He goes through the double doors and exits upstage the front hall followed by **TOLEDO**. **SYLVESTER** watches them leave, then looks up at **STURDYVANT** in the control booth, looks around the empty room, crosses to the piano stool and sits. [Lights: The studio slowly dims as lights fade up in the bandroom.] **SLOW DRAG** is playing solitaire on the downstage right bench. **LEVEE**, on the upstage center bench, polishes his cornet. **CUTLER** is sitting, drowsily, in the downstage left chair.)*

LEVEE. Slow Drag, you ever been to New Orleans?

SLOW DRAG. What's in New Orleans that I want?

LEVEE. How you call yourself a musician and ain't never been to New Orleans?

SLOW DRAG. You ever been to Fat Back, Arkansas?

> *(**LEVEE** shakes his head.)*

Alright, then. Ain't never been nothing in New Orleans that I couldn't get in Fat Back.

LEVEE. That's why you backwards. You just an old country boy talking about Fat Back, Arkansas and New Orleans in the same breath.

CUTLER. I been to New Orleans. What about it?

LEVEE. You ever been to Lula White's?

CUTLER. Lula White's? I ain't never heard of it.

(**SLOW DRAG** *gathers the playing cards and puts them in his vest pocket.*)

LEVEE. Man, they got some gals in there just won't wait! I seen a man get killed in there once. Got drunk and grabbed one of the gals wrong... I don't know what the matter of it was. (*Rises and crosses toward* **CUTLER.**) But he grabbed her and she stuck a knife in him all the way up to the hilt. He ain't even fell. He just stood there and choked on his own blood. (*Picks up the piano chair, carries it to upstage left of* **SLOW DRAG** *and sits on it.*) I was just asking Slow Drag 'cause I was gonna take him to Lula White's when we get down to New Orleans and show him a good time. Introduce him to one of them gals I know down there.

(**SLOW DRAG** *snorts.*)

CUTLER. Slow Drag don't need you to find him no pussy. He can take care of his ownself. (*Humorously.*) Fact is... you better watch your gal when Slow Drag's around. They don't call him Slow Drag for nothing. (*Rises and crosses to left of* **LEVEE.**) Tell him how you got your name Slow Drag.

SLOW DRAG. I ain't thinking about Levee.

CUTLER. Slow Drag break a woman's back when he dance. (*Mimes* **SLOW DRAG** *dancing with an imaginary partner.*) They had this contest one time in this little town called Bolingbroke about a hundred miles outside Macon. We was playing for this dance and they was giving twenty dollars to the best Slow Draggers. (*Mimes* **SLOW DRAG** '*s dance, again.*) Slow Drag looked over the competition, got down off the bandstand, grabbed hold of one of them gals and stuck to her like a fly to jelly. Like wood to glue. Man had the gal whooping and hollering so... everybody stopped to watch. This fellow come in...this gal's fellow...and pulled a knife a foot long on Slow Drag. *(Mimes the "fellow" pulling an imaginary knife and glaring at* **SLOW DRAG.***)* 'Member that, Slow Drag?

SLOW DRAG. *(Chuckles.)* Boy, that mama was hot! The front of her dress was wet as a dishrag!

LEVEE. *(Excitedly.)* So what happened? What the man do?

CUTLER. Slow Drag ain't missed a stroke. *(Dances with the imaginary partner.)* The gal, she just look at her man with that sweet dizzy look in her eye. She ain't about to stop! Folks was clearing out, ducking and hiding under tables, figuring there's gonna be a fight. *(Ducks behind* **LEVEE,** *then steps right and resumes his dance.)* Slow Drag just looked over the gal's shoulder at the man and said... "Mister, if you'd quit hollering and wait a minute...you'll see I'm doing you a favor. I'm helping this gal win ten dollars so she can buy you a gold watch." *(Stops and mimes the "fellow," stroking a long imaginary knife.)* The man just stood there and looked at him, all the while stroking that knife. Told Slow Drag, say "Alright then, nigger. You just better make damn sure you win." *(All laugh as* **CUTLER** *crosses above* **LEVEE** *to right of* **SLOW DRAG** *and sits on the downstage right bench.)* That's when folks started calling him Slow Drag. The women got to hanging around him so bad after that, them fellows in that town ran us out of there.

> *(***TOLEDO** *opens the Bandroom door, enters, carrying a small cardboard box, and closes the door.)*

LEVEE. Yeah...well, them gals in Lula White's will put a harness on his ass.

TOLEDO. *(Drops the box on top of the piano and crosses to upstage left of* **LEVEE.***)* Ma's up there. Some kind of commotion with the police.

CUTLER. *(Starts.)* Police? What the police up there for?

TOLEDO. I couldn't get it straight. Something about her car. They gone now...she's alright. Mr. Irvin sent some sandwiches. (*Gestures toward the piano as* LEVEE *leaps up, crosses to the piano and grabs the box.*)

LEVEE. Yeah, alright. What we got here? (*Crosses to the upstage center bench, sits and greedily takes two sandwiches wrapped in wax paper from the box.*)

TOLEDO. (*Indignantly.*) What you doing grabbing two? There ain't but five in there...how you figure you get two?

LEVEE. Cause I grabbed them first.

> (TOLEDO *takes the box out of* LEVEE*'s hand and crosses to above* CUTLER.)

There's enough for everybody...what you talking about? It ain't like I'm taking food out of nobody's mouth.

> (TOLEDO *offers the box to* CUTLER.)

CUTLER. That's alright. He can have mine too. I don't want none.

TOLEDO. (*He crosses to above* SLOW DRAG; LEVEE *leaps toward the box.* TOLEDO *shoves* LEVEE *away as* SLOW DRAG *takes a sandwich from the box.*) Nigger, you better get out of here. (*Offers the box to* SLOW DRAG *again.*) Slow Drag, you want this?

SLOW DRAG. Naw, you can have it. (*Unwraps his sandwich.*)

TOLEDO. (*Picks up the piano chair and places it at the piano as* LEVEE *sits on the upstage center bench and unwraps a sandwich.*) With Levee around, you don't have to worry about no leftovers. I can see that. (*Takes a sandwich, drops the box on the downstage left chair and sits at the piano.*)

LEVEE. What's the matter with you? Ain't you eating two sandwiches?

> (TOLEDO *unwraps his sandwich;* SLOW DRAG *starts to eat.*)

Then why you wanna talk about me? Talking about there won't be no leftovers with Levee around. Look at your ownself before you look at me.

TOLEDO. That's what you is. That's what we all is. A leftover from history. You see now, I'll show you... *(Puts his sandwich on the piano and turns toward* **CUTLER** *and* **SLOW DRAG.***)*

LEVEE. Aw, shit... I done got the nigger started now. *(Turns away from* **TOLEDO** *and begins to devour his sandwich.)*

TOLEDO. Now I'm gonna show you how this goes...where you just a leftover from history. Everybody come from different places in Africa, right? Come from different tribes and things. Soonawhile they began to make one big stew. You had the carrots, the peas, and potatoes and what not over here. And over there, you had the meat, the nuts, the okra, corn...and then you mix it up and let it cook right through to get the flavors flowing together...then you got one thing. You got a stew.

Now you take and eat the stew. You take and make your history with that stew. Alright. Now it's over. Your history's over and you done ate the stew. But you look around and you see some carrots over here, some potatoes over there. That stew's still there. You done made your history and it's still there. You can't eat it all. So what you got? You got some leftovers. That's what it is. You got some leftovers and you can't do nothing with it. You already making you another history... cooking you another meal, and you don't need them leftovers no more. What to do?

See, we's the leftovers. The colored man is the leftovers. Now what's the colored man gonna do with himself? That's what we waiting to find out. But first we gotta know we the leftovers.

Now, who knows that? You find me a nigger that knows that and I'll turn any which-a-way you want me to. I'll bend over for you. You ain't gonna find that. And that's what the problem is. The problem ain't with the white

man. The white man know you just a leftover. 'Cause
he the one who done the eating and he know what he
done ate. But we don't know that we been took and
made history out of. Done went and filled the white
man's belly and now he's full and tired and wants you to
get out the way and let him be by himself. Now, I know
what I'm talking about. And if you wanna find out, you
just ask Mr. Irvin what he had yesterday for supper.
And if he's an honest white man...which is asking for
a whole heap of a lot...he'll tell you he done ate your
black ass and if you please, I'm full up with you...so go
on and get off the plate and let me eat something else.
(Turns to the piano and picks up his sandwich.)

SLOW DRAG. *(Bewildered.)* What that mean? What's eating
got to do with how the white man treat you? He don't
treat you no different according to what he ate.

TOLEDO. I ain't said it had nothing to do with how he treat
you. *(Begins eating his sandwich.)*

CUTLER. The man's trying to tell you something, fool!

SLOW DRAG. What he trying to tell me? Ain't you here?
Why you say he was trying to tell me something? Wasn't
he trying to tell you, too?

LEVEE. He was trying alright. He was trying a whole heap.
I'll say that for him. But trying ain't worth a damn. I
got lost right there trying to figure out who puts nuts in
their stew. *(Finishes his sandwich and tosses the wax paper
upstage right.)*

SLOW DRAG. I knowed that before. My grandpappy used to
put nuts in his stew. He and my grandma both. That
ain't nothing new.

TOLEDO. They put nuts in their stew all over Africa. But the
stew they eat, and the stew your grandpappy made, and
all the stew that you and me eat, and the stew Mr. Irvin
eats...ain't in noway the same stew. That's the way that
go. I'm through with it. That's the last you know me to
ever try and explain something to you.

CUTLER. *(Rises, sighs and crosses toward the downstage left chair.)* Well, time's getting along...come on, let's finish rehearsing.

> *(***TOLEDO*** *picks up the sandwich box and puts it on top of the piano.* ***CUTLER*** *sits on the downstage left chair.* ***SLOW DRAG*** *crumples his wax paper, puts it in his pocket, crosses to the crates and picks up his bass.)*

LEVEE. *(Puts his cornet and the second sandwich in the case under the bench and stretches out on his back, lazily.)* I don't feel like rehearsing. I ain't nothing but a leftover. You go and rehearse with Toledo...he's gonna teach you how to make a stew.

SLOW DRAG. Cutler, what you gonna do? I don't want to be around here all day.

LEVEE. I know my part. You all go on and rehearse your part. You all need some rehearsal.

CUTLER. Come on, Levee, get up off your ass and rehearse the songs.

LEVEE. I already know them songs...what I wanna rehearse them for?

SLOW DRAG. You in the band ain't you? You supposed to rehearse when the band rehearse.

TOLEDO. *(Playfully.)* Levee think he the King of the Barnyard. He thinks he's the only rooster know how to crow.

LEVEE. Alright! Alright!

> *(***TOLEDO*** *grins at* ***CUTLER*** *as* ***LEVEE*** *jumps up and grabs his cornet.)*

Come on. I'm gonna show you I know them songs. Come on, let's rehearse. I bet you the first one mess up be Toledo. Come on... I wanna see if he know how to crow.

CUTLER. "Ma Rainey's Black Bottom," Levee's version. Let's do it. A-One. A-Two. You know what to do.

> *(The band mimes playing as [Lights: the Bandroom dims as lights fade up in the Studio.] SYLVESTER is sitting at the piano and STURDYVANT is arranging his files in the control booth.)*

MA RAINEY. *(Singing accappella, from off right.)*
OH LORD, THESE DOGS OF MINE
THEY SURE DO WORRY ME ALL THE TIME.

> *(She enters the Front Hall carrying one shoe and wearing the other as DUSSIE MAE follows languidly behind her. MA opens the upstage double door and crosses into the Studio.)*

THEY REASON WHY, I DON'T KNOW
LORD, I BEG TO BE EXCUSED
I CAN'T WEAR ME NO SHARP-TOED SHOES

> *(MA crosses to the right folding chair, sits and drops her purse on the left chair. DUSSIE MAE crosses to above MA and rests a hand on MA's shoulder.)*

I WENT FOR A WALK
I STOPPED TO TALK
OH, HOW MY CORNS DID BARK.

> *(MA laughs loudly and rubs her foot as DUSSIE MAE crosses to downstage right and looks around the Studio. SYLVESTER plunks a few high notes on the piano.)*

DUSSIE MAE. It feels kinda spooky in here. I ain't never been in no recording studio before. *(SYLVESTER plunks a few lower notes.)* Where's the band at?

MA RAINEY. They off somewhere rehearsing. I don't know where Irvin went to.

> *(SYLVESTER hits a few notes further down the keyboard as MA takes off the other shoe and puts both shoes under her chair.)*

All this hurry up and he goes off back there with Sturdyvant.

> *(SYLVESTER hits a few low keys.)*

I know he better come on 'cause Ma ain't gonna be waiting.

> (**SYLVESTER** *pounds a few notes at the bottom of the keyboard as* **MA** *turns to look at* **DUSSIE MAE.**)

Come here...let me see that dress.

> (**DUSSIE MAE** *crosses to right of* **MA** *and turns, showing off the dress.* **MA** *touches the dress, approvingly.*)

That dress looks nice. I'm gonna take you tomorrow and get you some more things before I take you down to Memphis. They got clothes up here you can't get in Memphis. I want you to look nice for me. If you gonna travel with the show, you got to look nice.

DUSSIE MAE. *(Crosses to the cane chair, sits, puts her purse under the chair and rubs her foot.)* I need me some more shoes. These hurt my feet.

MA RAINEY. You get you some shoes that fit your feet. Don't you be messing around with no shoes that pinch your feet. Ma know something about bad feet. *(Gestures toward* **SYLVESTER.**)* Hand me my slippers out my bag over yonder.

> (**DUSSIE MAE** *rises and starts toward* **SYLVESTER** *as he jumps up, takes a pair of slippers out of the bag, crosses to left of* **MA** *and kneels.*)

DUSSIE MAE. *(She crosses back to the cane chair, sits and glares at* **SYLVESTER.** *He tucks the bag under one arm and puts* **MA**'s *slippers on her feet.)* I just want to get a pair of them yellow shoes. About a half size bigger.

MA RAINEY. We'll get you whatever you need.

> (**SYLVESTER** *rises and stands attentively, left of* **MA,** *his shirt tail hanging out of his pants.*)

Sylvester, too... I'm gonna get him some more clothes *(Looks at* **SYLVESTER**'s *shirt tail.)* Sylvester...tuck your clothes in. Straighten them up and look nice. Look like a gentleman.

(SYLVESTER *looks at his clothes, hurriedly tucks in
the shirt and straightens his coat.*)

DUSSIE MAE. *(Scornfully.)* Look at Sylvester with that hat on.

MA RAINEY. Sylvester, take your hat off inside. Act like your
mama taught you something.

(SYLVESTER *glares at* DUSSIE MAE, *takes his hat
off, crosses over the platform, and right around*
DUSSIE MAE *to the piano.*)

I know she taught you better than that.

(SYLVESTER *sits at the piano.*)

Come on over here and leave that piano alone.

SYLVESTER. I ain't d-d-doing nothing to the p-p-piano. I'm
just l-l-looking at it.

MA RAINEY. Well. Come on over here and sit down.

(SYLVESTER *rises obediently, crosses to the chair
left of* MA *and sits, holding the bag and his hat
on his lap.*)

As soon as Mr. Irvin comes back, I'll have him take you
down and introduce you to the band.

(DUSSIE MAE *stretches out one leg, lifts her skirt
and adjusts her stocking garters.* IRVIN *enters
down the front hall, comes through double doors
and crosses into the Studio.* IRVIN *stops and stares
silently at* DUSSIE MAE'*s leg as the door swings
shut.*)

He's gonna take you down there and introduce you
in a minute...have Cutler show you how your part go.
And when you get your money you gonna send some of
it home to your mama. Let her know you doing alright.
Make her feel good to know you doing alright in the
world.

(DUSSIE MAE *turns right and glances at* IRVIN.
*She picks up her purse, rises, straightens her skirt
and crosses to upstage left.*)

IRVIN. *(Crosses a step toward* MA.*)* Ma, I called down to the garage and checked on your car. It's just a scratch. They'll have it ready for you this afternoon. They're gonna send it over with one of their fellows.

MA RAINEY. They better have my car fixed right, too. I ain't going for that.

> *(DUSSIE MAE opens the left door and looks down the back hall as the band lifts their instruments and [MUSIC: The band plays LEVEE's version of the "BLACK BOTTOM," quietly.])*

Brand new car...they better fix it like new.

IRVIN. It was just a scratch on the fender, Ma...

> *(MA cocks her ear towards the door, listening to the faint sound of the band, then turns to DUSSIE MAE. DUSSIE MAE swings her hips and snaps her fingers to the music.)*

They'll take care of it...don't worry...they'll have it like new.

> *(MA looks disapprovingly at DUSSIE MAE. DUSSIE MAE glances at MA, then crosses away to the piano stool.)*

MA RAINEY. Irvin...what is that I hear? What is that the band's rehearsing? I know they ain't rehearsing Levee's "Black Bottom." I know I ain't hearing that.

IRVIN. Ma, listen... *(Turns the cane chair backwards and sits facing MA; casually:)* That's what I wanted to talk to you about... Levee's version of that song...it's got a nice arrangement...a nice horn intro...it really picks it up...

MA RAINEY. *(Crossly.)* I ain't studying Levee nothing. I know what he done to that song and I don't like to sing it that way. I'm doing it the old way. That's why I brought my nephew to do the voice intro.

IRVIN. Ma...that's what the people want now. *(Rises and crosses toward the radiator; persuasively:)* They want something they can dance to. Times are changing.

Levee's arrangement gives the people what they want.
It gets them excited...makes them forget about their
troubles.

MA RAINEY. I don't care what you say, Irvin. Levee ain't
messing up my song. If he got what the people want...
let him take it somewhere else. I'm singing Ma Rainey's
song. I ain't singing Levee's song. Now that's all there
is to it. Carry my nephew on down there and introduce
him to the band.

(SYLVESTER *rises, hopefully.*)

I promised my sister I'd look out for him and he's
gonna do the voice intro on the song my way.

IRVIN. (*Crosses to the cane chair and sits.*) Ma...we just figured
that...

MA RAINEY. (*Irritated.*) Who's this "we"? What you mean
"we"? You and Sturdyvant? You and Levee? Who's "we"?
I ain't studying Levee nothing. Come talking this "we"
stuff. Who's "we"?

IRVIN. Me and Sturdyvant. We decided that it would...

MA RAINEY. You decided, huh? I'm just a bump on the log.
I'm gonna go which ever way the river drift. Is that it?
You and Sturdyvant decided.

IRVIN. Ma. It was just that we thought it would be better.

MA RAINEY. (*Ironically.*) I ain't got good sense. I don't know
nothing about music. I don't know what's a good song
and what ain't. You know more about my fans than I
do.

IRVIN. (*Pleadingly.*) It's not that, Ma. It would just be easier
to do. It's more what the people want.

MA RAINEY. (*Exasperated.*) I'm gonna tell you something,
Irvin...and you go on up there and tell Sturdyvant.
What you all say don't count with me. You understand?
Ma listens to her heart. Ma listens to the voice inside
her. That's what counts with Ma. Now, you carry my
nephew on down there...tell Cutler he's gonna do the
voice intro on that Black Bottom song...and that Levee

ain't messing up my song with none of his music shit. Now, if that don't set right with you and Sturdyvant... then I can carry my black bottom on back down south to my tour, 'cause I don't like it up here no ways.

IRVIN. Okay, Ma... I don't care. I just thought...

MA RAINEY. *(Angrily.)* Damn what you thought! What you look like telling me how to sing my song? This Levee and Sturdyvant nonsense... I ain't going for it! *(Turns to* SYLVESTER.*)* Sylvester, go on down there and introduce yourself. I'm through playing with Irvin.

SYLVESTER. *(Runs out the left door, turns right into the closet, then crosses back to the left doorway; flustered:)* Which way you go? Where they at?

MA RAINEY. *(Rises and crosses to right of* SYLVESTER.*)* Here... I'll carry you down there myself.

DUSSIE MAE. *(Rises; expectantly:)* Can I go? I wanna see the band.

MA RAINEY. *(Curtly.)* You stay your behind up here. Ain't no cause in you being down there. *(She starts toward the back hall.* DUSSIE MAE *sits on the piano stool.)* Come on, Sylvester.

IRVIN. *(Rises, resigned.)* Okay, Ma. Have it your way. We'll be ready to go in fifteen minutes.

MA RAINEY. *(Turns back into the studio; haughtily:)* We'll be ready to go when Madame says we're ready. That's the way it goes around here.

> *(*MA *crosses into the back hall followed by* SYLVESTER. *He closes the door. Simultaneously: [Lights: The Studio dims as the lights fade up in the Bandroom;* MUSIC: *The band plays louder;] as* IRVIN *goes through the double doors and exits upstage the front hall;* STURDYVANT *comes down the staircase and follows* IRVIN *out.* DUSSIE MAE *watches* IRVIN *and* STURDYVANT *exit, then follows after them.* LEVEE *crosses to downstage center as he plays.* MA *opens the Bandroom door and crosses slowly toward* LEVEE. SYLVESTER *follows* MA *into*

the Bandroom and crosses to above the piano.
CUTLER *glances at* **MA,** *[MUSIC:* **CUTLER** *drops out followed by* **TOLEDO.***]* **CUTLER** *rises and looks at* **MA** *sheepishly.* **SLOW DRAG** *glances toward* **MA** *and [MUSIC:* **SLOW DRAG** *drops out.]* **SLOW DRAG** *tries to get* **LEVEE***'s attention.* **LEVEE** *looks downstage right and continues to play.* **MA** *crosses to left of* **LEVEE** *and glares at him disparagingly.* **LEVEE** *glances toward* **MA** *[MUSIC:* **LEVEE** *stops playing] and crosses upstage right.)*

(Continued; turns to **CUTLER***; dryly:)* Cutler…this here is my nephew, Sylvester. He's gonna do that voice intro on the Black Bottom song using the old version.

LEVEE. *(Crosses to* **MA***; angrily:)* What you talking about? Mr. Irvin said he's using my version. What you talking about?

MA RAINEY. *(Coldly.)* Levee, I ain't studying you or Mr. Irvin.

*(***LEVEE** *crosses upstage right.)*

Cutler…get him straightened out on how to do his part. I ain't thinking about Levee. These folks done messed with the wrong person this day. Sylvester, Cutler gonna teach you your part. *(To* **SYLVESTER,** *patiently.)* You go ahead and get it straight. Don't worry about what nobody else say.

(She crosses into the back hall and closes the door. Everyone is silent for a moment. **SYLVESTER** *looks around the room.)*

CUTLER. *(Resigned.)* Well, come on in, boy.

*(***SYLVESTER** *crosses hesitantly to below the upstage center bench.* **CUTLER** *picks up his trombone.)*

I'm Cutler. You got Slow Drag…

*(***SLOW DRAG** *smiles and waves.)*

Levee…

(**LEVEE** *growls, crosses to the downstage right chair and sits.* **CUTLER** *turns to the left and gestures toward* **TOLEDO.**)

And that's Toledo over there.

(**TOLEDO** *nods at* **SYLVESTER.**)

Sylvester, huh?

SYLVESTER. Sylvester Brown.

LEVEE. *(Snarls to himself.)* I done wrote a version of that song what picks it up and sets it down in the people's lap! Now she come talking this! You don't need that old circus bullshit! I know what I'm talking about. You gonna mess up that song, Cutler, and you know it.

CUTLER. I ain't gonna mess up nothing. Ma say…

LEVEE. *(Turns to* **CUTLER***; abruptly:)* I don't care what Ma say! I'm talking about what the intro gonna do to the song. The peoples in the North ain't gonna buy all that tent show nonsense. They wanna hear some music!

CUTLER. Nigger, I done told you time and again…you just in the band. You plays the piece…whatever they want! Ma says what to play! Not you! You ain't here to be doing no creating. Your job is to play whatever Ma says.

LEVEE. I might not play nothing! I might quit!

CUTLER. Nigger, don't nobody care if you quit. Who's heart you gonna break?

TOLEDO. Levee ain't gonna quit. He got to make some money to keep him in shoe polish.

(*All laugh except* **LEVEE** *and* **SYLVESTER.**)

LEVEE. I done told you all…you all don't know me. You don't know what I'll do.

CUTLER. I don't think nobody too much give a damn *(Turns to* **SYLVESTER.***)* Sylvester…here's the way your part go. The band plays the intro… I'll tell you where to come in. The band plays the intro and then you say… Alright boys, you done seen the rest… Now I'm gonna show you the best… Ma Rainey's gonna show you her Black

Bottom. You got that? *(Crosses to the downstage left chair and sits.)* Let me hear you say it one time.

SYLVESTER. *(Breathes deeply.)* Alright boys, you d-d-done seen the rest, n-n-now I'm gonna show you the best. M-M-M-M-M-M-Ma Rainey's gonna s-s-show you her black b-b-bottom. *(He looks at* **CUTLER**, *expectantly.* **CUTLER** *nods and smiles.)*

LEVEE. *(Dumbfounded, turns slowly to* **SYLVESTER**, *then explodes.)* What kind of...alright, Cutler! Let me see you fix that! You straighten that out! You hear that shit, Slow Drag? How in the hell the boy gonna do the part and he can't even talk!

SYLVESTER. *(Crosses a step toward* **LEVEE**, *boldly.)* W-W-W-Who's you tell me what to do, nigger! This ain't you band. Ma tell me to d-d-d-do it and I'm gonna do it. You can go to hell, n-n-n-nigger!

LEVEE. *(Slowly rises, facing* **SYLVESTER**.*)* B-B-B-Boy, ain't nobody studying you. You go on and fix that one, Cutler. *(Crosses to the crates, disgustedly.)* You fix that one and I'll... I'll shine your shoes for you! You go on and fix that one!

TOLEDO. You say you Ma's nephew, huh?

SYLVESTER. *(Defensively.)* Yeah. So w-w-w-what that mean?

TOLEDO. Oh, I ain't meant nothing... I was just asking.

SLOW DRAG. *(Turns his face away from* **SYLVESTER** *and tries to stifle a laugh.)* Well, come on and let's rehearse so the boy can get it right.

LEVEE. I ain't rehearsing nothing! *(Crosses to the downstage right chair and sits.)* You just wait till I get my band. I'm gonna record that song and show you how it supposed to go!

CUTLER. We can do it without Levee. Let him sit on over there. Sylvester, you remember your part?

SYLVESTER. I remember it pretty g-g-good.

CUTLER. Well, come on, let's do it then. One. Two. You know what to do.

(LEVEE sulks as [MUSIC: TOLEDO plays a brief piano introduction, then CUTLER and SLOW DRAG join in on "MA RAINEY'S BLACK BOTTOM."] STURDYVANT opens the Bandroom door and crosses to upstage right of the piano, smiling broadly.)

STURDYVANT. Good...you boys are rehearsing, I see.

([MUSIC: The band stops playing] as LEVEE jumps up and crosses to STURDYVANT.)

LEVEE. *(Enthusiastically.)* Yessir! We rehearsing. We know them songs real good.

STURDYVANT. Good! Say... Levee...did you finish that song?

LEVEE. Yessir, Mr. Sturdyvant. *(Takes two sheets of music from the horn case under the bench; confidently:)* I got it right here. I wrote that other part just like you say. It go like:

You can shake it, you can break it

You can dance at any hall

You can slide across the floor

You'll never have to stall

My jelly, my roll, sweet mama don't you let it fall.

(Turns to the second sheet of music.) Then I put that part in there for the people to dance, like you say, for them to forget about their troubles.

STURDYVANT. Good! Good! I'll just take this. *(Takes both sheets of music from LEVEE's hand and smiles.)* I wanna see you about your songs as soon as I get the chance. *(Crosses to the bandroom door.)*

LEVEE. Yessir! As soon as you get the chance, Mr. Sturdyvant.

(STURDYVANT exits and closes the door. LEVEE paces excitedly upstage as the men stare at him.)

CUTLER. You hear Levee? You hear this nigger? "Yessuh, we's rehearsing boss."

SLOW DRAG. *(Mockingly.)* I heard him. Seen him, too. Shuffling them feet.

TOLEDO. Aw, Levee can't help it none. He's like all of us. Spooked up with the white man.

LEVEE. *(Stops and glares.)* I'm spooked up with him alright. You let one of them crackers fix on me wrong. I'll show you how spooked up I am with him.

TOLEDO. That's the trouble of it. You wouldn't know if he was fixed on you wrong or not. You so spooked up by him, you ain't had the time to study him.

LEVEE. *(Resentfully.)* I studies the white man. I got him studied good. The first time one fixes on me wrong, I'm gonna let him know just how much I studied him. Come telling me I'm spooked up by the white man. You let one mess with me... I'll show you how spooked up I am.

CUTLER. You talking out your hat. The man come in here, call you a boy, tell you to get up off your ass and rehearse...and you ain't had nothing to say to him, 'cepting "Yessir!"

LEVEE. *(Crosses a step toward* **CUTLER**.*)* I can say "yessir" to whoever I please. What you got to do with it? I know how to handle white folks. I been handling them for thirty-two years, and now you're gonna tell me how to do it. Just 'cause I say "yessir" don't mean I'm spooked up by him. I know what I'm doing. Let me handle him my way.

CUTLER. Well, go on and handle it then.

LEVEE. Toledo, you always messing with somebody! Always agitating somebody with that old philosophy bullshit you be talking. You stay out of my way about what I do and say. I'm my own person. Just let me alone.

TOLEDO. You right, Levee. I apologize. It ain't none of my business... *(Turns to* **CUTLER** *and smirks.)* ...that you spooked up by the white man.

(**CUTLER** *and* **SLOW DRAG** *laugh.*)

LEVEE. *(Warningly.)* Alright! See! That's the shit I'm talking about. You all back up and leave Levee alone.

SLOW DRAG. Aw, Levee, we was all just having fun. Toledo ain't said nothing about you he ain't said about me. You just taking it all wrong.

TOLEDO. *(Appeasingly.)* I ain't meant nothing by it, Levee. *(Turns to* **CUTLER.***)* Cutler, you ready to rehearse.

LEVEE. *(Paces angrily, right of* **TOLEDO.***)* Levee got to be Levee! And he don't need nobody messing with him about the white man—'cause you don't know nothing about me. You don't know Levee. You don't know nothing about what kind of blood I got! What kind of heart I got beating here! I was eight years old when I watched a gang of white mens come into my daddy's house and have to do with my mama anyway they wanted. Never will forget it.

We was living in Jefferson County, about eighty miles outside of Natchez. My daddy's name was Memphis... Memphis Lee Green...had him near fifty acres of good farming land. I'm talking good land! Grow anything you want! He done gone off of shares and bought this land from Mr. Hallie's widow-woman after he done passed on. Folks called him an uppity nigger 'cause he done saved and borrowed to where he could buy this land and be independent.

It was coming on planting time and my daddy went into Natchez to get him some seed and fertilizer. Called me, say, Levee, you the man of the house now. Take care of your mama while I'm gone. I wasn't but a little boy, eight years old.

My mama was frying up some chicken when them mens come in that house. Must have been eight or nine of them. She was standing there frying that chicken and them mens come and took hold of her just like you take hold of a mule and make him do what you want.

There was my mama with a gang of white mens. She tried to fight them off, but I could see where it wasn't

gonna do her any good. I didn't know what they were
doing to her...but I figured whatever it was they may
as well do to me, too. My daddy had a knife that he
kept around there for hunting and working and what
not. I knew where he kept it and I went and got it.
*(Crosses to the downstage right bench and puts his cornet on
the bench.)* I'm gonna show you how spooked up I was
by the white man. I tried my damnedest to cut one of
them's throat! I hit him on the shoulder with it. *(Crosses
to below the upstage center bench.)* He reached back and
grabbed hold of that knife and whacked me across the
chest with it. *(Pulls up his shirt and exposes a long, ugly
scar on his chest.)* That's what made them stop. They was
scared I was gonna bleed to death. My mama wrapped
a sheet around me and carried me two miles down to
the Furlow place and they drove me up to Doc Albans.
He was waiting on a calf to be born and said he ain't
had time to see me. They carried me up to Miss Etta,
the midwife, and she fixed me up.

My daddy came back and acted like he done accepted
the facts of what happened. But he got the names of
them white men from my mama. He found out who
they was and then we announced we was moving out
of the county. Said good-bye to everybody...all the
neighbors. My daddy went and smiled in the face of
one of them crackers who had been with my mama.
Smiled in his face and sold him our land. We moved
over with relations in Caldwell. He got us settled in and
then he took off one day. I ain't never seen him since.
He sneaked back hiding up in the woods, laying to get
them eight or nine men.

He got four of them before they got him. They tracked
him down in the woods. Caught up with him, hung
him and set him afire. *(Turns to the silver cornet on the
bench.)* My daddy wasn't spooked up by the white man.
Nosir! And that taught me how to handle them. *(Slowly
crosses to the cornet, lifts it and clutches it tightly to his chest,
grief-stricken.)* I seen my daddy go up and grin in this

cracker's face...smile in his face and sell him his land. All the while he's planning how he's gonna get him and what he's gonna do to him. That taught me how to handle them. So you all just back up and leave Levee alone about the white man. I can smile and say "yessir" to whoever I please *(Crosses to the upstage center bench, subdued.)* I got my time coming to me. You all just leave Levee alone about the white man. *(Sits on the left end on the bench, facing upstage.)*

SLOW DRAG. *([MUSIC:* **SLOW DRAG** *starts a slow, rhythmic beat on the body of the bass.] Singing:)*

IF I HAD MY WAY

IF I HAD MY WAY

IF I HAD MY WAY

([MUSIC: **SLOW DRAG** *stops the rhythmic beat.])*

I WOULD TEAR THIS OLD BUILDING DOWN.

([Lights: The stage fades quickly to black.] After a moment, [Lights: a dim glow warms the front hall, the studio and the bandroom.] After a few moments, [Sound: Intermission music begins: female vocalist renditions of blues songs.])

ACT TWO

([Sound: A female vocal rendition of **"TRUST NO
MAN."** *Lights: The stage fades to black. Sound:
The song ends.] A single note is heard repeatedly
on a piano. [Lights: The bandroom lights fade
up to a dim glow as the studio lights fade up
brightly] revealing* **MA** *at the studio piano singing
quietly and playing a single note; and* **DUSSIE
MAE** *seated in the right folding chair, holding
her purse.* **STURDYVANT** *opens the left door and
enters the Studio followed by* **CUTLER** *carrying his
guitar case and trombone,* **TOLEDO, SLOW DRAG**
carrying his bass, **LEVEE** *carrying his cornet,
and* **SYLVESTER** *carrying his hat and* **MA** *'s bag.*
STURDYVANT *crosses to the microphone, moves
it right a few inches, then crosses up the spiral
staircase to the Control Booth as* **MA** *crosses to the
mic.* **CUTLER** *places his guitar case behind the
left door and crosses to downstage right* **TOLEDO**
crosses to the piano and sits on the stool. **SLOW
DRAG** *crosses below* **TOLEDO** *and stands right of
the piano.* **SYLVESTER** *crosses to the upstage left
stool and sits.* **LEVEE** *crosses to the left folding
chair, eyeing* **DUSSIE MAE.** **MA** *nods approvingly
at the placement of her microphone, crosses through
the double doors into the Front Hall as* **IRVIN**
*enters down the Front Hall and crosses through
the double doors into the Studio.* **MA** *sings softly in
the Front Hall.* **LEVEE** *sits on the left folding chair.*
CUTLER *motions to* **IRVIN,** *then* **IRVIN** *crosses to
right of* **CUTLER.** *)*

CUTLER. *(Quietly.)* Mr. Irvin, I don't know what you gonna
do. I ain't got nothing to do with it, but the boy can't do

the part. He stutters. He can't get it right. He stutters right through it every time…

IRVIN. Christ! Okay. We'll…shit! We'll just do it like we planned. We'll do Levee's version. I'll handle it, Cutler. Come on, let's go. I'll think of something.

> (IRVIN *crosses to the double doors and knocks on the window. He crosses to the spiral staircase, climbs to the top of the stairs, pulls the drape across the stairwell, then enters the Control Booth and closes the door.* CUTLER *starts to cross toward* TOLEDO *as* MA *comes through the double doors and steps into the Studio. She looks at* LEVEE; *he is staring at* DUSSIE MAE's *leg.*)

MA RAINEY. Cutler. (CUTLER *crosses to left of* MA.) Levee's got his eyes in the wrong place. You better school him, Cutler.

CUTLER. (*Crosses toward* LEVEE.) Come on, Levee…let's get ready to play!

> (LEVEE *rises.* CUTLER *glares at him. Emphatically:*)

Get your mind on your work!

> (LEVEE *crosses above* DUSSIE MAE *to right of* SLOW DRAG. MA *picks up the upstage right stool and moves it to left of the radiator. She taps the stool and stares at* DUSSIE MAE. DUSSIE MAE *rises obediently, crosses to the stool and sits.*)

IRVIN. (*Into the booth mic.*) Okay, boys…we're gonna do Moonshine Blues first. Moonshine Blues, Ma.

MA RAINEY. (*Crosses to the platform, muttering loudly.*) I ain't doing no Moonshine nothing. I'm doing the Black Bottom first. Come on, Sylvester.

> (SYLVESTER *rushes to* MA's *microphone.* MA *turns to the Control Booth.*)

Where's Sylvester's mic? You need a mic for Sylvester. (*Takes* SYLVESTER *by the arm and pushes him toward left of* DUSSIE MAE.) Irvin…get him a mic.

IRVIN. *(Into the booth mic.)* Uh… Ma…the boys say he can't do it.

MA RAINEY. *(Crosses to her mic and speaks into it, testily.)* Who say he can't do it? What boys say he can't do it?

IRVIN. *(Into the booth mic.)* The band, Ma…the boys in the band.

MA RAINEY. *(Into her mic.)* What band? The band work for me! I say what goes! *(Turns to* **CUTLER.***)* Cutler, what's he talking about? *(Turns to* **LEVEE** *suspiciously.)* Levee, this some of your shit?

IRVIN. *(Into the booth mic.)* He stutters, Ma. They say he stutters.

MA RAINEY. *(Turns back to her mic.)* I don't care if he do. I promised the boy he could do the part…and he's gonna do it! That's all there is to it. He don't stutter all the time. Get a microphone down here for him.

IRVIN. *(Into the booth mic.)* Ma…we don't have time. We can't…

MA RAINEY. *(Into her mic.)* If you wanna make a record you gonna find time. I ain't playing with you, Irvin. I can walk out of here and go back to my tour. I got plenty fans. I don't need to go through all of this. Just go and get the boy a microphone.

> *(***STURDYVANT** *and* **IRVIN** *confer quietly in the control booth for a moment, then* **IRVIN** *opens the door and climbs down the spiral staircase.)*

STURDYVANT. *(Into the booth mic.)* Alright, Ma…we'll get him a microphone. But if he messes up…he's only getting one chance…the cost…

> *(***IRVIN** *crosses below* **SLOW DRAG** *to the left door, opens it and disappears into the closet.)*

MA RAINEY. *(Into her mic.)* Damn the cost. You always talking about the cost. I make more money for this outfit than anybody else you got put together. If he messes up he'll just do it till he gets it right.

(IRVIN reappears, carrying a microphone on a stand with a coiled cable, closes the left door and crosses toward SYLVESTER. MA turns to LEVEE.)

MA RAINEY. Levee... I know you had something to do with this. You better watch yourself.

(IRVIN places the microphone below SYLVESTER, uncoils the cable, crosses to the jack box upstage of the double doors and plugs it in.)

LEVEE. It was Cutler!

SYLVESTER. *(Turns on LEVEE.)* It was you! You the only one m-m-mad about it.

LEVEE. *(Crosses a step toward MA.)* The boy stutter. He can't do the part. Everybody see that. I don't know why you want the boy to do the part noways.

(IRVIN crosses to the spiral staircase, climbs up to the control booth, enters and closes the door.)

MA RAINEY. Well, can or can't...he's gonna do it! You ain't got nothing to do with it!

LEVEE. *(Disgusted.)* I don't care what you do! He can sing the whole goddamned song for all I care! *(Crosses to right of SLOW DRAG.)*

MA RAINEY. Well, alright. Thank you. *(Crosses to SYLVESTER.)* Come on, Sylvester.

(She takes the hat and bag out of SYLVESTER's hands and places them on the cane chair. SYLVESTER steps hesitantly toward the mic. Encouragingly:)

You just stand here and hold your hands like I told you.

(SYLVESTER assumes an opera singer's posture. Reassuringly:)

Just remember the words and say them...that's all there is to it. Don't worry about messing up. If you mess up we'll do it again. Now, let me hear you say it. *(Turns to CUTLER.)* Play it for him, Cutler.

CUTLER. One. Two. You know what to do.

> (*[**MUSIC:** **TOLEDO** plays a short piano intro, then the band begins to play "MA RAINEY'S BLACK BOTTOM."]* **SYLVESTER** rocks back and forth in front of the mic. **MA** smiles.*)

SYLVESTER. Alright, boys, you d-d-d-done s-s-s-seen the best...now I'm gonna show you the rest...

> (*[**MUSIC:** **SLOW DRAG** drops out, followed by **LEVEE.**]*)

Ma Rainey's gonna show you...

> (*[**MUSIC:** **CUTLER** drops out, followed by **TOLEDO.**]*)

...her b-b-black b-b-bottom.

> (*Everyone is silent as **SYLVESTER** looks hopefully at **MA.***)

MA RAINEY. (*Smiles broadly and crosses to **SYLVESTER.***) That's alright. That's real good. You take your time, you'll get it right.

STURDYVANT. (*Into the booth mic.*) Listen, Ma...now when you come in...don't wait so long to come in. Don't take so long on the intro, huh?

MA RAINEY. (*Tips **SYLVESTER**'s mic toward her and speaks into it.*) Sturdyvant, don't you go trying to tell me how to sing. You just take care of that up there and let me take care of this down here. (*Crosses to the platform and looks around the room, absently.*) Where's my Coke?

IRVIN. (*Into the booth mic.*) Okay, Ma. We're all set up to go up here. Ma Rainey's Black Bottom, boys

MA RAINEY. Where's my Coke. I need a Coke. You ain't got no Coke down here? Where's my Coke?

IRVIN. (*Into the booth mic.*) What's the matter, Ma? What's...

MA RAINEY. (*Into her mic.*) Where's my Coke? I need a Coca-Cola.

IRVIN. *(Into the booth mic, cajolingly.)* Uh… Ma…look… I forgot to get Coke, huh? Let's do it without it, huh? Just this one song. What say, boys?

MA RAINEY. *(Turns to the control booth and shouts.)* Damn what the band say! You know I don't sing nothing without my Coca-Cola!

STURDYVANT. *(He leaves the control booth, bounds down the spiral case and crosses to right of* MA. IRVIN *follows, patiently, outraged.)* Now, just a minute here, Ma. You come in an hour late…we're way behind schedule as it is… the band is set up and ready to go… I'm burning my lights… I've turned up the heat…we're ready to make a record and what? You decide you want a Coca-Cola?

MA RAINEY. *(Coldly.)* Sturdyvant, get out of my face. *(Turns to* IRVIN.*)* Irvin… I told you keep him away from me.

IRVIN. Mel, I'll handle it.

STURDYVANT. *(Turns to* IRVIN.*)* I'm tired of her nonsense, Irv. I'm not gonna put up with this!

IRVIN. Let me handle it, Mel. I know how to handle her.

> *(*IRVIN *crosses below* STURDYVANT *to right of* MA; SLOW DRAG *puts his bass on top of the piano.)*

Look, Ma… Ill call down to the deli and get you a Coke. But let's get started, huh? Sylvester's standing there ready to go…the band's set up…let's do this one song, huh?

> *(*STURDYVANT, *exasperated, crosses through the double doors and exits upstage the Front Hall.)*

MA RAINEY. *(Obstinately.)* If you too cheap to buy me a Coke… I'll buy my own. *(Turns to* SLOW DRAG.*)* Slow drag! Sylvester, go with Slow Drag and get me a Coca-Cola. *(Picks up her purse from the left folding chair, takes out a dollar bill and hands it to* SLOW DRAG.*)* Slow Drag, walk down to that store on the corner and get me three bottles of Coca-Cola.

(**SLOW DRAG** *crosses through the double doors, and exits upstage the front hall followed by* **SYLVESTER**. **MA** *turns to* **IRVIN**.)

Get out of my face, Irvin. You all just wait until I get my Coke. It ain't gonna kill you.

IRVIN. (*Grudgingly.*) Okay, Ma. Get your Coke, for Chrissakes! Get your Coke! (*He throws up his hands, crosses through the double doors and exits upstage the front hall.* **LEVEE** *crosses to the left door, opens it and exits into the back hall.* **TOLEDO** *crosses to the back hall.* **CUTLER** *leans his trombone against the piano and starts toward the left door.*)

MA RAINEY. (*Crosses to the cane chair.*) Cutler, come here a minute. I want to talk to you.

(**TOLEDO** *exits into the back hall, closing the door behind him.* **MA** *turns the cane chair toward downstage left and sits with her feet on the platform as* **CUTLER** *crosses reluctantly to the right folding chair and sits.*)

What's all this about "the boys in the band say"? I tells you what to do. I says what the matter is with the band. I say who can and can't do what.

(**LEVEE** *opens the bandroom door, enters, crosses to the upstage center bench and sits.* **TOLEDO** *follows* **LEVEE** *into the bandroom, crosses to the piano and sits.*)

CUTLER. We just say 'cause the boy stutter…

MA RAINEY. I know he stutters. Don't you think I know he stutters. This is what's gonna help him.

CUTLER. Well, how can he do the part if he stutters? You want him to stutter through it? We just thought it be easier to go on and let Levee do it like we planned.

(**DUSSIE MAE** *rises, carrying her purse, crosses quietly above* **CUTLER** *to the left folding chair. She picks up* **MA**'s *purse, sits and puts both purses under the chair.*)

MA RAINEY. I don't care if he stutters or not! He's doing the part and I don't wanna hear anymore of this shit about what the band says. And I want you to find somebody to replace Levee when we get to Memphis. Levee ain't nothing but trouble.

CUTLER. Levee's alright. He plays good music when he puts his mind to it. He knows how to write music, too.

(**DUSSIE MAE** *rises and crosses to* **MA***'s mic.*)

MA RAINEY. I don't care what he know. He ain't nothing but bad news. Find somebody else. I know it was his idea about who to say who can do what.

(**DUSSIE MAE** *fondles the mic, swings her hips and snaps her fingers rhythmically.* **CUTLER** *glances surreptitiously at* **DUSSIE MAE**. **MA** *looks at* **CUTLER**. *Curtly:*)

Dussie Mae, go sit your behind down somewhere and quit flaunting yourself around.

DUSSIE MAE. *(Resentfully.)* I ain't doing nothing.

MA RAINEY. *(Softens.)* Well, just go on somewhere and stay out the way.

(**DUSSIE MAE** *crosses sulkily to right of the left folding chair.*)

CUTLER. I been meaning to ask you, Ma...about these songs. This Moonshine Blues...

(**DUSSIE MAE** *bends over and picks up the purses.* **CUTLER** *glances uneasily at* **DUSSIE MAE***'s "behind" as it swings inches from his face.* **MA** *glares at* **CUTLER**.)

...that's one of them songs Bessie Smith sang, I believes.

(**DUSSIE MAE** *puts* **MA***'s purse on the left chair and crosses to the piano.*)

MA RAINEY. *(Indignantly.)* Bessie what? Ain't nobody thinking about Bessie. I taught Bessie. She ain't doing nothing but imitating me. What I care about Bessie? I don't care if she sell a million records. She got her people and I got mine. I don't care what nobody else do. Ma was the first and don't you forget it!

(**DUSSIE MAE** *sits on the piano stool and looks around the room.*)

CUTLER. Ain't nobody said nothing about that. I just said that's the same song she sang.

MA RAINEY. I been doing this a long time. Ever since I was a little girl. I don't care what nobody else do. That's what gets me so mad with Irvin. White folks try to be put out with you all the time. Too cheap to buy me a Coca-Cola. I lets them know it though. Ma don't stand for no shit. Wanna take my voice and trap it in them fancy boxes with all them buttons and dials...and then too cheap to buy me a Coca-Cola. And it don't cost but a nickle a bottle.

CUTLER. I knows what you mean about that.

(**DUSSIE MAE** *takes a nail file cut of her purse and files her nails.*)

MA RAINEY. They don't care nothing about me. All they want is my voice. Well, I done learned that and they gonna treat me like I want to be treated no matter how much it hurt them. They back there now calling me all kinds of names...calling me everything but a child of God. But they can't do nothing else. They ain't got what they wanted yet. As soon as they get my voice down on them recording machines, then it's just like if I'd be some whore and they roll over and put their pants on. Ain't got no use for me then. I know what I'm talking about. You watch. Irvin right there with the rest of them. He don't care nothing about me either. He been my manager for six years and the only time he had me in his house was to sing for some of his white friends.

CUTLER. I know how they do.

(**DUSSIE MAE** *slides off the piano stool, crosses quietly toward the left door, and opens it.*)

MA RAINEY. If you colored and can make them some money then you alright with them. Otherwise you just a dog in the alley.

(DUSSIE MAE *exits through the left door and shuts it.*)

I done made this company more money from my records than all the other recording artists they got put together. And they wanna balk about how much this session is costing them.

CUTLER. I don't see where it's costing them all what they say.

MA RAINEY. It ain't! I don't pay that kind of talk no mind.

(*[Lights: The studio dims as the bandroom lights fade up.]* LEVEE *is straddling the upstage center bench and working on a sheet of music.* TOLEDO, *seated at the piano, reads a newspaper.* DUSSIE MAE *opens the bandroom door a crack.*)

LEVEE. (*Singing.*)
YOU CAN SHAKE IT, YOU CAN BREAK IT.
YOU CAN DANCE AT ANY HALL
YOU CAN SLIDE ACROSS THE FLOOR
YOU'LL NEVER HAVE TO STALL
MY JELLY, MY ROLL, SWEET MAMA DON'T YOU LET IT FALL

(DUSSIE MAE *opens the door a bit further.*)

Wait till Mr. Sturdyvant hear me play that! I'm talking about some real music here, Toledo! I'm talking about real music! (*Glances at the Bandroom door.*) Hey, mama! Come on in. (*Takes a rag out of his case, puts his foot on the upstage center bench and polishes his shoe.*)

DUSSIE MAE. Oh, hi... I just wanna see what it looks like down here.

LEVEE. (*Drops the rag into his case and rises.*) Well, come on in... I don't bite.

DUSSIE MAE. (*Crosses to upstage right of the piano.*) I didn't know you could really write music. I thought you was just jiving me at the club last night.

LEVEE. Naw, baby... I knows how to write music. *(Picks up the cornet.)* I done give Mr. Sturdyvant some of my songs and he say he's gonna let me record them. Ask Toledo. I'm gonna have my own band! Toledo...ain't I give Mr. Sturdyvant some of my songs I wrote!

TOLEDO. *(Rises, drops the newspaper on the piano and starts toward the Bandroom door.)* Don't get Toledo mixed up in nothing.

> *(DUSSIE MAE steps into TOLEDO's path, smiles at him and after a moment, steps to the left TOLEDO crosses quickly to the Bandroom door, exits and closes the door.)*

DUSSIE MAE. *(Crosses to downstage right of the piano and drops her purse on the piano chair.)* You gonna get your own band, sure enough?

LEVEE. *(Crosses tentatively toward DUSSIE MAE and puts his cornet on the piano.)* That's right! Levee Green and His Foot-stompers.

> *(TOLEDO opens the left door, enters the Studio and closes the door. He crosses to the piano and sits.)*

DUSSIE MAE. That's real nice.

LEVEE. That's what I was trying to tell you last night. A man whats gonna get his own band need to have a woman like you.

DUSSIE MAE. A woman like me wants somebody to bring it and put it in my hand. I don't need nobody wanna get something for nothing and leave me standing in my door.

LEVEE. That ain't Levee's style, sugar. I got more style than that. I knows how to treat a woman. Buy her presents and things...treat her like she want to be treated.

DUSSIE MAE. That's what they all say...till it come time to be buying the presents.

LEVEE. When we get down to Memphis, I'm gonna show you what I'm talking about. I'm gonna take you out and show you a good time. Show you Levee know how to treat a woman.

DUSSIE MAE. *(Crosses to above the downstage right.)* When you getting your own band?

LEVEE. *(Follows* **DUSSIE MAE** *to the bench.)* Soon as Mr. Sturdyvant say. I done got my fellows already picked out. Getting me some good fellows know how to play real sweet music. *(Starts to put his arm around her waist.)*

DUSSIE MAE. *(Pushes his arm away and crosses away to upstage right.)* Go on now, I don't go for all that pawing and stuff. When you get your own band maybe we can see about this stuff you talking.

LEVEE. *(Crosses to left of the upstage center bench.)* I just want to show you I know what the women like. *(He crosses above the upstage center bench to* **DUSSIE MAE.** *She slowly backs away to the right.)* They don't call me Sweet Lemonade for nothing. (**LEVEE** *pursues her.)*

DUSSIE MAE. Stop it now! Somebody's gonna come in here.

LEVEE. *(Catches her, puts his arms around her waist and holds her tightly.)* Naw, they ain't. Look here, sugar…what I wanna know is…can I introduce my red rooster to your brown hen?

DUSSIE MAE. You get your band then we'll see if your rooster know how to crow.

LEVEE. *(Grins and pulls her in more tightly.)* Damn, baby! Now I know why my grandpappy sat on the back porch with his straight razor when my grandma hung out the wash.

DUSSIE MAE. Nigger, you crazy!

LEVEE. I bet you sound like the midnight train from Alabama when it crosses the Mason Dixon line.

DUSSIE MAE. How'd you get so crazy?

LEVEE. It's women like you…drives me that way.

> *(He pulls her tighter to him and kisses her.* **DUSSIE MAE** *jerks away toward upstage left* **LEVEE** *grabs her wrist and stops her. He slowly sits on the upstage center bench, staring at her, then releases her wrist. She crosses hesitantly toward him. [Lights: The Bandroom dims as the Studio lights come up.]* **DUSSIE MAE** *kisses* **LEVEE** *and sinks*

onto his lap as **MA,** *in the Studio, looks around and sighs.)*

MA RAINEY. It sure done got quiet in here. I never could stand no silence. I always got to have some music going on in my head somewhere. It keeps things balanced. Music will do that. It fills things up. The more music you got in the world, the fuller it is.

CUTLER. I can agree with that. I got to have my music, too.

MA RAINEY. White folks don't understand about the blues. They hear it come out but they don't know how it got there.

They don't understand that's life's way of talking. You don't sing to feel better. You sing 'cause that's a way of understanding life.

CUTLER. That's right. You get that understanding and you done got a grip on life to where you can hold your head up and go on to see what else life got to offer.

MA RAINEY. The blues help you get out of bed in the morning. You get up knowing you ain't alone. *(Crosses left a step.)* There's something else in the world. Something's been added by that song. This be an empty world without the blues. I take that emptiness and try to fill it up with something.

TOLEDO. *(Rises and crosses to the left folding chair.)* You fill it up with something the people can't be without, Ma. That's why they call you the Mother of the Blues. *(Picks up* **MA***'s purse and sits on the left folding chair.)* You fill up that emptiness in a way ain't nobody ever thought of doing before. And now they can't be without it.

MA RAINEY. I ain't started the blues way of singing. The blues always been here.

CUTLER. In the church sometimes you find that way of singing. They got blues in the church.

MA RAINEY. They say I started it...but I didn't. I just helped it out. Filled up that empty space a little bit. That's all. But if they wanna call me the Mother of the Blues, that's alright with me. It don't hurt none.

(**SLOW DRAG** *enters down the front hall and bursts through the double doors followed by* **SYLVESTER.** **SLOW DRAG,** *shivering, carries a paper bag;* **SYLVESTER,** *his collar turned up and his hat on his heady still carries* **MA**'s *bag.*)

MA RAINEY. It sure took you long enough. That store ain't but on the corner.

SLOW DRAG. (*Crosses to left of* **MA** *and kneels; takes a Coke and a bottle opener out of the paper bag, opens the bottle and hands it to* **MA.**) That one was closed. We had to find another one. (*He drops the opener and the bottle cap in the bag and shoves the bag under* **CUTLER**'s *chair, rises, crosses to the left door, exits into the Back Hall and closes the door.* **MA** *takes a long drink of the Coke.*)

MA RAINEY. (*Over her shoulder, to* **SYLVESTER.**) Sylvester, go and find Mr. Irvin and tell him we ready to go.

(**SYLVESTER** *goes through the double doors and exits upstage the Front Hall. [Lights: The Studio dims slightly as the Bandroom lights fade up.]* **SLOW DRAG** *opens the Bandroom door, surprising* **LEVEE** *and* **DUSSIE MAE.** *She springs off* **LEVEE**'s *lap and turns to* **SLOW DRAG.**)

SLOW DRAG. Cold out.

(**DUSSIE MAE** *relaxes and crosses to downstage right of the piano.*)

I just wanted to warm up with a little sip.

(*He crosses to the open locker, takes out the bourbon bottle, opens it and drinks.* **LEVEE** *stares hungrily at* **DUSSIE MAE.** **TOLEDO** *rises, crosses to the Studio piano and sits on the stool.*)

Ma got her Coke, Levee. We about ready to start.

(**SLOW DRAG** *crosses to the Bandroom door, pushes it wide open, looks back into the room for a moment and exits into the Back Hall.* **LEVEE,** *still staring at* **DUSSIE MAE,** *rises and starts toward* *her.* **CUTLER** *rises, crosses to the Studio piano and picks up his trombone.)*

DUSSIE MAE. *(Picks up her purse.)* No... Come on! I got to go. You gonna get me in trouble.

(She exits swiftly into the Back Hall. **LEVEE** *starts to follow her, stops in the doorway and stares after her.* **SLOW DRAG** *opens the left door, enters the Studio, closes the door, crosses to right of the piano and takes down his bass.)*

LEVEE. *(Crosses into the piano and picks up his cornet.)* Good God! Happy Birthday to the lady with the cakes.

([Lights: The Bandroom dims as the Studio lights fade up.] **LEVEE** *exits into the Back Hall and closes the Bandroom door.* **STURDYVANT** *enters down the Front Hall and crosses through the double doors into the Studio, closely followed by* **IRVIN** *and* **SYLVESTER.** **IRVIN** *and* **STURDYVANT** *cross to the spiral staircase, climb up to the Control Booth, enter and close the door.* **SYLVESTER** *stands just inside the double doors.* **DUSSIE MAE** *opens the left door, enters the Studio, closes the door, then crosses to* **MA.** *She kisses* **MA** *lightly on the cheek, crosses the stool downstage right and sits.)*

IRVIN. *(Into the Booth mic.)* We're all set up here, Ma. We're all set to go. You ready down there?

MA RAINEY. *(She rises and turns to* **SYLVESTER.** *He puts his hat and bag on the cane chair and crosses to his mic.)* Sylvester, you just remember your part and you say it. That's all there is to it.

*(***SYLVESTER** *looks anxiously at the mic and pulls at his tie as* **MA** *crosses calmly over to the platform and speaks into her mic.)*

Yeah, we ready.

*(***LEVEE** *opens the left door, enters the Studio, closes the door and crosses hurriedly to right of* **SLOW**

DRAG. MA *glares at* LEVEE. *He glances at* DUSSIE MAE.*)*

IRVIN. *(Flips a switch downstage of the Control Booth door. [Lights: The red "recording" light comes on over the double doors.] Into the Booth mic:)* Okay, boys. "Ma Rainey's Black Bottom." Take one.

CUTLER. A-One. A-Two. You know what to do.

([MUSIC: TOLEDO plays a brief piano introduction, then the band plays "MA RAINEY'S BLACK BOTTOM."])

SYLVESTER. *(Lurches toward the mic and pulls at his tie.)* Alright boys, you d-d-done seen…

([MUSIC: The band quickly drops out.])

IRVIN. *(Shouts into the Booth mic.)* Hold it!

(STURDYVANT takes a disc off the recording machine and replaces it with a new disc. He nods at IRVIN. *Into the Booth mic:)*

Take two.

CUTLER. A-One. A-Two. You know what to do.

([MUSIC: TOLEDO plays the introduction, then the band plays "MA RAINEY'S BLACK BOTTOM."])

SYLVESTER. *(Lurches again toward the mic and pulls at his tie.)* Alright boys, you done seen the rest…now I'm gonna show you the best. Ma Rainey's g-g-g-gonna… *(Rushing.)* …show you her black bottom!

IRVIN. *(Into the Booth mic.)* Hold it! Hold it!

([MUSIC: The band drops out,] reluctantly. STURDYVANT *takes the disc off of the recording machine and replaces it with another one.* IRVIN *sighs. Into the Booth mic:)*

Take three. Ma…let's do it without the intro, huh? No voice intro…just come in singing.

MA RAINEY. Irvin, I done told you...the boy's gonna do the part. He don't stutter all the time...just give him a chance. *(Crosses to left of* **SYLVESTER** *and takes his tie out of his hands.)* Sylvester...hold your hands like I told you and just relax. Just relax and concentrate.

> *(She crosses back to the platform and nods at* **IRVIN**. **SYLVESTER** *assumes the opera singer's posture.)*

IRVIN. *(Into the Booth mic.)* Alright. Take three.

CUTLER. A-One. A-Two. You know what to do.

> *([MUSIC:* **TOLEDO** *plays the introduction, then the band plays* "MA RAINEY'S BLACK BOTTOM."] **SYLVESTER** *stands stiffly in front of his mic.* **IRVIN** *and* **STURDYVANT** *cross their fingers.)*

SYLVESTER. Alright boys, you done seen the rest...now, I'm gonna show you the best. Ma Rainey's gonna show you her black bottom.

> *(**SYLVESTER** looks at* **MA**, *amazed.* **IRVIN** *and* **STURDYVANT** *cheer silently in the Control Booth.* **MA** *smiles broadly, then steps up to her mic.)*

MA RAINEY. *(Singing.)*
WAY DOWN SOUTH IN ALABAMY
I GOT A FRIEND THEY CALL DANCING SAMMY
WHO'S CRAZY ABOUT ALL THE LATEST DANCES
BLACK BOTTOM STOMPING, TWO BABIES PRANCING

THE OTHER NIGHT AT A SWELL AFFAIR
AS SOON AS THE BOYS FOUND OUT THAT I WAS THERE
THEY SAID, COME ON MA, LET'S GO TO THE CABARET
WHEN I GOT THERE YOU OUGHT TO HEAR THEM SAY

I WANT TO SEE THE DANCE YOU CALL THE BLACK BOTTOM
I WANT TO LEARN THAT DANCE
I WANT TO SEE THE DANCE YOU CALL YOUR BIG BLACK
    BOTTOM
IT'LL PUT YOU IN A TRANCE

ALL THE BOYS IN THE NEIGHBORHOOD
THEY SAY YOUR BLACK BOTTOM IS REALLY GOOD
COME ON AND SHOW ME YOUR BLACK BOTTOM
I WANT TO LEARN THAT DANCE

I WANT TO SEE THE DANCE YOU CALL THE BLACK BOTTOM
I WANT TO LEARN THAT DANCE
COME ON AND SHOW THE DANCE YOU CALL YOUR BIG
 BLACK BOTTOM
IT PUTS YOU IN A TRANCE

EARLY LAST MORNING ABOUT THE BREAK OF DAY
GRANDPA TOLD MY GRANDMA, I HEARD HIM SAY
GET UP AND SHOW YOUR OLD MAN YOUR BLACK BOTTOM
I WANT TO LEARN THAT DANCE

> (**MA** *slaps her hips as [**MUSIC:** the band plays a
> short instrumental break.]*)

I DONE SHOWED Y'ALL MY BLACK BOTTOM
YOU OUGHT TO LEARN THAT DANCE.

> (*Everyone is silent for a moment.* **STURDYVANT**
> *lifts the needle from the recording disc.*)

IRVIN. (*Into the Booth mic.*) Okay, that's good, Ma. That
sounded great. Good job, boys.

> (*He flips the recording light switch to off. [Lights:
> The recording light over the double doors goes off]*
> **IRVIN** *opens the Control Booth door and climbs
> down the spiral staircase. Everyone bursts into
> congratulations and cheers.*)

MA RAINEY. (*Crosses to right of* **CUTLER.**) See! I told you. I
knew you could do it. (*Turns to* **SYLVESTER.**) You just
have to put your mind to it. Didn't he do good, Cutler?
Sound real good. I told him he could do it. (*Crosses to*
SYLVESTER.)

CUTLER. He sure did. He did better than I thought he was
gonna do.

> (**SYLVESTER** *smiles broadly.*)

IRVIN. *(He picks up **SYLVESTER**'s mic, moves it upstage right a few feet, and starts toward the spiral staircase. **MA** smiles happily and crosses back to her mic.)* Okay, boys... Ma... let's do Moonshine Blues next, huh? Moonshine Blues, boys.

STURDYVANT. *(Into the Booth mic.)* Irv! Something's wrong down there. We don't have it right.

IRVIN. *(Crosses to right of **MA** and speaks into her mic.)* What? What's the matter? Mel...

STURDYVANT. *(Shouts into the Booth mic.)* We don't have it right. Something happened. We don't have the goddamn song recorded!

IRVIN. *(Patiently.)* What's the matter? Mel, what happened? You sure you don't have nothing?

STURDYVANT. *(Into the Booth mic.)* Check that mic, huh, Irv.

> *(**IRVIN** reaches for **MA**'s mic. Sharply, into the Booth mic:)*

No. It's the kid's mic. Something's wrong with the mic. We've got everything all screwed up here.

IRVIN. *(Turns right and throws up his hands.)* Christ almighty! *(Turns to **MA**; quietly:)* Ma...we got to do it again. We don't have it. We didn't record the song. *(Crosses to **SYLVESTER**'s mic and traces the mic cable to the jack box.)*

MA RAINEY. What you mean you didn't record it? What was you and Sturdyvant doing up there?

IRVIN. *(Holds up the jack.)* Here... Levee must have kicked the plug out. *(Coils the cable.)*

LEVEE. I ain't done nothing! I ain't kicked nothing!

SLOW DRAG. If Levee had his mind on what he's doing...

MA RAINEY. Levee, if it ain't one thing it's another. You better straighten yourself up!

LEVEE. *(Crosses toward **MA** a step.)* Hell...it ain't my fault. I ain't done nothing!

STURDYVANT. *(Into the Booth mic.)* What's the matter with that mic? Irv? What's the problem?

IRVIN. *(Waves the jack at the Control Booth)* It's the cord, Mel. The cord's all chewed up. We need another cord. *(Picks up the mic, crosses to the left door, opens it and exits into the closet.)*

MA RAINEY. *(Explodes.)* This is the most disorganized... Irvin, I'm going home! Come on, Dussie.

> *(She crosses through the double doors into the Front Hall, gets her coat and DUSSIE MAE's coat. STURDYVANT leaves the Control Booth and rushes down the staircase. IRVIN enters through the left Door, closes it and stands upstage left.)*

STURDYVANT. *(Crosses to right of IRVIN; furiously:)* Where's she going?

IRVIN. *(Smiles faintly.)* She said she's going home.

STURDYVANT. Irvin...you get her! If she walks out of here...

MA RAINEY. *(Comes through the double doors, drops DUSSIE MAE's coat onto her lap, then starts to put on her own coat.)* Come on, Sylvester.

IRVIN. Ma... Ma...listen. *(Crosses below STURDYVANT to left of MA and helps her with her coat.)* Fifteen minutes. All I ask is fifteen minutes!

MA RAINEY. Come on, Sylvester...get your coat.

STURDYVANT. *(Threateningly)* Ma...if you walk out of this studio...

IRVIN. Fifteen minutes, Ma!

STURDYVANT. You'll be through...washed up! If you walk out on me...

IRVIN. *(Turns to STURDYVANT: loudly:)* Mel, for Chris- sakes, shut up and let me handle it! *(Turns to MA; calmly:)* Ma, listen. These records are gonna be hits! They're gonna sell like crazy! Hell, even Sylvester will be a star. Fifteen minutes. That's all I'm asking! Fifteen minutes.

MA RAINEY. *(Looks at IRVIN, then at STURDYVANT; sternly:)* Fifteen minutes! You hear me, Irvin? Fifteen minutes... and then I'm gonna take my black bottom on back down to Georgia. Fifteen minutes. Then Madame Rainey is leaving!

IRVIN. *(He kisses* MA *on the cheek. She stares at him in astonishment. Jubilantly:)* Alright, Ma...fifteen minutes. I promise. *(Turns upstage, to the band.)* You boys go ahead and take a break. Fifteen minutes and we'll be ready to go.

> *(He crosses through the double doors and exits upstage the Front Hall followed by* STURDYVANT. TOLEDO *opens the left door and exits into the Back Hall, followed by* LEVEE. MA *takes off her coat, hands it to* DUSSIE MAE, *crosses to* SYLVESTER *and takes a large feather fan from his bag. She crosses to the right folding chair and sits.* SLOW DRAG *puts his bass on top of the piano.)*

CUTLER. *(Leans his trombone on the piano.)* Slow Drag, you got any of that bourbon left?

SLOW DRAG. Yeah, there's some down there.

> *(*CUTLER *crosses through the left door and exits into the Back Hall, followed by* SLOW DRAG. SLOW DRAG *closes the left door as [Lights: The Studio dims and the Bandroom lights fade up.]* DUSSIE MAE *crosses through the double doors into the Front Hall and hangs up the coats.* SYLVESTER *crosses to the piano stool and sits.* MA *gently fans herself.* TOLEDO *opens the Bandroom door, crosses to the piano chair and sits.* LEVEE *enters the Bandroom, crosses to the upstage center bench, stretches out on his back with his head toward* TOLEDO *and the cornet resting on his chest.* DUSSIE MAE *crosses back into the Studio and sits on the downstage right stool.* CUTLER *enters the Bandroom, followed by* SLOW DRAG. CUTLER *crosses to* SLOW DRAG*'s locker and takes out the bourbon bottle.)*

CUTLER. I could use a little nip. *(Opens the bottle, takes a drink, closes it and returns it to the locker.)*

SLOW DRAG. *(Crosses to the downstage right chair and sits.)* Don't make me no difference if she leave or not. I was kinda hoping she would leave.

CUTLER. *(Crosses to the downstage left chair and sits.)* I'm like Mr. Irvin…after all this time we done put in here, it's best to go ahead and get something out of it.

TOLEDO. Ma gonna do what she want to do, that's for sure. If I was Mr. Irvin, I'd best go on and get them cords and things hooked up right. And I wouldn't take no longer than fifteen minutes doing it.

CUTLER. *(Reprovingly.)* If Levee had his mind on his work we wouldn't be in this fix. We'd be up there finishing up. Now we got to go back and see if that boy get that part right. Ain't no telling if he ever get that right again in his life.

LEVEE. Hey, Levee ain't done nothing!

SLOW DRAG. Levee up there got one eye on the gal and the other on his trumpet.

CUTLER. *(Rises and crosses to left of* **LEVEE.** *)* Nigger, don't you know that's Ma's gal?

LEVEE. I don't care whose gal it is. I ain't done nothing to her. I just talk to her like I talk to anybody else.

CUTLER. *(Crosses to above* **LEVEE.** *)* Well, that being Ma's gal and that being that boy's gal is one and two different things. The boy is liable to kill you, but your ass gonna be out here scraping the concrete looking for a job if you messing with Ma's gal.

LEVEE. How am I messing with her? I ain't done nothing to the gal. I just asked her her name. Now, if you telling me I can't do that…then Ma will just have to go to hell.

CUTLER. All I can do is warn you.

SLOW DRAG. Let him hang himself, Cutler. Let him string his neck out.

LEVEE. I ain't done nothing to the gal! You all talk like I done went and done something to her. Leave me go with my business.

CUTLER. *(Crosses to right of* **LEVEE.** *)* I'm through with it. Try and talk to a fool… *(Crosses back to the downstage left chair and sits.)*

TOLEDO. *(Turns to* **SLOW DRAG.***)* Some mens got it worse than others...this foolishness I'm talking about. Some mens is excited to be fools. That excitement is something else. I knows about it. I done experienced it. It makes you feel good to be a fool. But it don't last long. It's over in a minute. Then you got to tend with the consequences. You got to tend with what comes after. That's when you wish you had learned something about it.

LEVEE. *(Cranes his neck and grins at* **TOLEDO.***)* That's the best sense you made all day. Talking about being a fool. That's the only sensible thing you said today. Admitting you was a fool.

TOLEDO. I admit it, alright. Ain't nothing wrong with it. I done been a little bit of everything.

LEVEE. Now you're talking. You as big a fool as they make.

TOLEDO. Gonna be a bit more things before I'm finished with it. Gonna be foolish again. But I ain't never been the same fool twice. I might be a different kind of fool, but I ain't gonna be the same fool twice. That's where we part ways.

SLOW DRAG. Toledo, you done been a fool about a woman?

TOLEDO. Sure. Sure I have. Same as everybody.

SLOW DRAG. Hell, I ain't never seen you mess with no woman. I thought them books was your woman.

TOLEDO. Sure I messed with them. Done messed with a whole heap of them. And gonna mess with some more. But I ain't gonna be no fool about them. What you think? I done come in the world full grown with my head in a book? I done been young. Married. Got kids. I done been around and I done loved women to where you shake in your shoes just at the sight of them. Feel it all up and down you spine.

SLOW DRAG. I didn't know you was married.

TOLEDO. Sure. Legally. I been married legally. Got the papers and all. I done been through life. Made my marks. Followed some signs on the road. Ignored some others. I done been all through it. I touched and been touched by it. But I ain't never been the same fool twice. That's what I can say.

LEVEE. But you been a fool. That's what counts. Talking about I'm a fool for asking the gal her name and here you is one yourself.

TOLEDO. Now, I married a woman. A good woman. To this day I can't say she wasn't a good woman. I can't say nothing bad about her. I married that woman with all the good graces and intentions of being hooked up and bound to her for the rest of my life. I was looking for her to put me in my grave.

But you see…it ain't all the time what your intentions and wishes are. She went out and joined the church. Alright. There ain't nothing wrong with that. A good Christian woman going to church and wanna do right by her God. There ain't nothing wrong with that. But she got up there, got to seeing them good Christian mens and wondering why I ain't like that. Soon she figure she got a heathen on her hands. She figured she couldn't live like that. The church was more important than I was. So she left. Packed up one day and moved out. To this day I ain't never said another word to her. Come home one day and my house was empty! And I sat down and figured out that I was a fool not to see that she needed something that I wasn't giving her. Else she wouldn't have been up there at the church in the first place. I ain't blaming her. I just said it wasn't gonna happen to me again. So yeah, Toledo been a fool about a woman. That's part of making life.

CUTLER. Well, yeah, I been a fool, too.

> (**LEVEE** *sits up and chuckles. He takes a rag out of his case and polishes his cornet.*)

Everybody done been a fool once or twice. But you see, Toledo, what you call a fool, and what I call a fool, is two different things. I can't see where you was being a fool for that. You ain't done nothing foolish. You can't

help what happened, and I wouldn't call you a fool for
it.

(LEVEE holds the cornet up and looks into the bell.)

A fool is responsible for what happens to him. A fool
cause it to happen. Like Levee...

*(LEVEE looks away from the cornet and scowls at
CUTLER.)*

...if he keep messing with Ma's gal and his feet be out
there scraping the ground. That's a fool.

LEVEE. Ain't nothing gonna happen to Levee. Levee ain't
gonna let nothing happen to him. Now, I'm gonna say
it again. I asked the gal her name. That's all I done.
And if that's being a fool...then you are looking at the
biggest fool in the world...cause I sure as hell asked
her.

SLOW DRAG. You just better not let Ma see you ask her.
That's what the man's trying to tell you.

LEVEE. I don't need nobody to tell me nothing.

CUTLER. Well, Toledo, all I gots to say is that from the looks
of it, from your story... I don't think life did you fair.

TOLEDO. Oh, life is fair. It's just in the taking what it gives
you.

LEVEE. Life ain't shit. You can put it in a paper bag and
carry it around with you. It ain't got no balls. Now,
death...death got some style! Death will kick your ass
and make you wish you never been born! That's how
bad death is! But you can rule over life. Life ain't
nothing.

*(SLOW DRAG looks right and puts his feet on the
downstage right bench.)*

TOLEDO. *(TOLEDO turns to CUTLER.)* Cutler, how's your
brother doing?

CUTLER. Who, Nevada? Oh, he's doing alright. Staying in
St. Louis. Got a bunch of kids last I heard.

TOLEDO. Me and him was alright with each other. Done a lot of farming together down in Plattsville.

CUTLER. Yeah, I know you all was tight. He in St. Louis now. Running an elevator last I hear about it.

SLOW DRAG. *(Turns to* CUTLER.*)* That's better than stepping in muleshit.

TOLEDO. Oh, I don't know now. I liked farming. Get out there in the sun…smell that dirt. Be out there by yourself…nice and peaceful. Yeah, farming was alright by me. Sometimes I think I'd like to get me a little old place…but I done got too old to be following behind one of them balky mules now.

LEVEE. Nigger talking about life is fair. And ain't got a pot to piss in.

TOLEDO. See, now, I'm gonna tell you something. A nigger gonna be dissatisfied no matter what. Give a nigger some bread and butter…and he'll cry cause he ain't got no jelly. Give him some jelly and he'll cry cause he ain't got no knife to put it on with. If there's one thing done learned in this life…it's that you can't satisfy a nigger no matter what you do. A nigger's gonna make his own dissatisfaction.

LEVEE. Niggers got a right to be dissatisfied. Is you gonna be satisfied with a bone somebody done throwed you when you see them eating the whole hog?

TOLEDO. You lucky they let you be an entertainer. They ain't got to accept your way of entertaining. You lucky and don't even know it. You's entertaining and the rest of the people is hauling wood. That's the only kind of job for the colored man.

SLOW DRAG. Ain't nothing wrong with hauling wood. I done hauled plenty wood. My daddy used to haul wood. Ain't nothing wrong with that. That's honest work.

LEVEE. *(Puts his cornet in the case under the bench.)* That ain't what I'm talking about. I ain't talking about hauling no wood. I'm talking about being satisfied with a bone somebody done throwed you. That's what's the matter with you all. You satisfied...sitting in one place. You got to move on down the road from where you sitting... and all the time you got to keep an eye out for the devil who's looking to buy up souls. And hope you get lucky and find him!

CUTLER. I done told about that blasphemy. Talking about selling your soul to the devil.

TOLEDO. We done the same thing, Cutler. There ain't no difference. We done sold Africa for the price of tomatoes. We done sold ourselves to the white man in order to be like him. Look at the way you dressed...that ain't African. That's the white man. We trying to be just like him. We done sold who we are in order to become someone else. We's imitation white men.

CUTLER. What else we gonna be living over here?

LEVEE. I'm Levee. Just me. I ain't no imitation nothing!

SLOW DRAG. You can't change who you are by how you dress. That's what I got to say.

TOLEDO. It ain't how you dress. It's how you act, how you see the world. It's how you follow life.

LEVEE. It don't matter what you talking about. I ain't no imitation white man. And I don't want to be no white man. *(Rises, arrogantly.)* As soon as I got my band together and make them records like Mr. Sturdyvant done told me I can make, I'm gonna be like Ma and tell the white man just what he can do. Ma tell Mr. Irvin she leavin'...and Mr. Irvin get down on his knees and beg her to stay! That's the way I'm gonna be! Make the white man respect me! *(Sits on the upstage left bench.)*

CUTLER. The white man don't care nothing about Ma. The colored folks made Ma a star. White folks don't care nothing about who she is...what kind of music she make.

SLOW DRAG. That's the truth about that. You let her go down to one of them white folks hotels and see how big she is.

CUTLER. Hell, she ain't got to do that. She can't even get a cab up here in the North. I'm gonna tell you something, *(Rises and crosses to downstage left of* LEVEE.*)* Reverend Gates...you know Reverend Gates? Slow Drag know who I'm talking about. Reverend Gates... now, I'm gonna show you how this go where the white man don't care a thing about who you is. Reverend Gates was coming from Tallahassee to Atlanta, going to see his sister who was sick at that time with the consumption. The train come up through Thomasville, then past Moultrie, and stopped in this little town called Sigsbee...

LEVEE. *(Emphatically.)* You can stop telling that right there! That train don't stop in Sigsbee. I know what train you talking about. That train got four stops before it reach Macon to go on to Atlanta. One in Thomasville, one in Moultrie, one in Cordele...and it stop in Centerville.

CUTLER. Nigger, I know what I'm talking about. You gonna tell me where the train stop?

LEVEE. Hell, yeah, if you talking about it stop in Sigsbee. I'm gonna tell you the truth.

CUTLER. *(Increasingly agitated.)* I'm talking about this train! I don't know what train you been riding. I'm talking about this train!

LEVEE. Ain't but one train. Ain't but one train come out of Tallahassee heading north to Atlanta and it don't stop at Sigsbee. Tell him, Toledo...that train don't stop at Sigsbee. The only train that stops at Sigsbee is the Santa Fe, and you have to transfer at Moultrie to get it!

CUTLER. Well, hell, maybe that's what he done! I don't know! I'm just telling you the man got off the train at Sigsbee!

LEVEE. Alright...you telling it. Tell it your way. Just make up anything.

SLOW DRAG. *(Rises, crosses to the downstage left chair and sits)* Levee, leave the man alone and let him finish.

CUTLER. I ain't paying Levee no never mind.

LEVEE. Go on tell it your way.

CUTLER Anyway... Reverend Gates got off this train in Sigsbee. *(Glances testily at* **LEVEE**, *then crosses to right of* **TOLEDO**.*)* The train done stopped there and he figured he'd get off and check the schedule to be sure he arrive in time for somebody to pick him up. Alright. While he's there checking the schedule, it come upon him that he had to go to the bathroom. Now, they ain't had no colored restrooms at the station. The only colored restroom is an outhouse they got sitting way back two hundred yards or so from the station. Alright. He in the outhouse and the train go off and leave him there. He don't know nothing about this town. Ain't never been there before—in fact, ain't never even heard of it before.

LEVEE. *(Jumps up, impatiently.)* I heard of it! I know just where it's at...and he ain't got off no train coming out of Tallahassee in Sigsbee! *(Crosses to the downstage right chair and sits.)*

CUTLER. The man standing there trying to figure out what he's gonna do...where this train done left him in this strange town. It started getting dark. He see where the sun's getting low in the sky, and he's trying to figure out what he's gonna do, when he noticed a couple of white fellows standing across the street from this station. Just standing there watching him. And then two or three more come up and joined the other ones. He look around, ain't seen no colored folks nowhere. He didn't know what was gettin in these here fellows minds, so he started walkin. *(Walking in place.)* He ain't knowed where he was going. He just walking down the railroad tracks when he hear them call him, "Hey, nigger!" See, just like that, "Hey, nigger!" He kept on walking. They call him some more and he just keep walking. Just going on down the tracks. And then he heard a gunshot where somebody done fired a gun in the air. *(Makes a loud explosive noise.)* He stopped then, you know.

TOLEDO. You don't even have to tell me no more. I know the facts of it. I done heard the same story a hundred times. It happened to me, too. Same thing.

CUTLER. Naw, I'm gonna show you how the white folks don't care nothing about who or what you is. They crowded around him. These gang of mens made a circle around him. Now, he's standing there, you understand...got his cross around his neck like them preachers wear. Had his little bible with him what he carry all the time. So they crowd on around him and one of them ask who he is. He told them he was Reverend Gates and that he was going to see his sister who was sick and the train left without him. And they said, "Yeah, nigger...but can you dance?" He looked at them and commenced to dancing. *(Hesitates a moment, then does a slow shuffle.)* One of them reached up and tore his cross off his neck. Said he was committing a heresy by dancing with a cross and bible. Took his bible and tore it up and had him dancing till they got tired of watching him.

SLOW DRAG. White folks ain't never had no respect for the colored minister.

CUTLER. That's the only way he got out of there alive... was to dance. Ain't even had no respect for a man of God! Wanna make him into a clown. Reverend Gates sat right in my house and told me that story from his own mouth. *(Crosses to upstage left of LEVEE; emphatically:)* So...the white folks don't care nothing about Ma Rainey. She's just another nigger who they can use to make some money. *(Glares at LEVEE a moment, then crosses to the upstage center bench and sits.)*

LEVEE. What I wants to know is...if he's a man of God... then where the hell was God when all of this was going on? Why wasn't God looking out for him? Why didn't God strike down them crackers with some of this lightning you talking about to me?

CUTLER. Levee, you gonna burn in hell.

LEVEE. What I care about burning in hell? You talking like a fool…burning in hell. Why didn't God strike some of them crackers down? Tell me that! That's the question! Don't come telling me this burning in hell shit! He a man of God…why didn't God strike some of them crackers down? I'll tell you why! I'll tell you the truth! It's sitting out there as plain as day! 'Cause he a white man's God. That's why! God ain't never listened to no nigger's prayers. *(Rises and crosses to downstage left of* CUTLER.*)* God take a nigger's prayers and throw them in the garbage. God don't pay niggers no mind. In fact, God hate niggers! Hate them with all the fury in his heart. Jesus don't love you. Jesus hate your black ass! *(Turns downstage and crosses back to the downstage right bench.)* Come talking that shit to me. Talking about burning in hell! *(Turns to* CUTLER*; tauntingly:)* God can kiss my ass.

CUTLER. *(He leaps toward* LEVEE *and punches him on the jaw.* LEVEE *reels backwards and falls over the downstage right.)* You worthless…that's my God! That's my God! That's my God! You wanna blaspheme my God!

> *(*CUTLER *starts toward* LEVEE *as* LEVEE *sprawls on the floor downstage right of the bench.* TOLEDO *and* SLOW DRAG *grab* CUTLER *and hold him back.)*

SLOW DRAG. Come on, Cutler…let it go! It don't mean nothing!

CUTLER. Wanna blaspheme my God! You worthless… talking about my God!

LEVEE. *(Scrambles to his feet, reaches into his pocket, pulls out a large pocketknife, opens it and flashes it at* CUTLER.*)* Naw, let him go! Let him go!

> *(*TOLEDO *and* SLOW DRAG *release* CUTLER *and step away;* TOLEDO *crosses to upstage right and* SLOW DRAG *crosses to downstage left of the piano.)*

LEVEE. That's your God, huh? That's your God, huh? Is that right? Your God, huh? Alright.

(CUTLER *backs upstage right as* LEVEE *crosses left around the downstage right bench and waves the knife at* CUTLER.)

LEVEE. I'm gonna give your God a chance. I'm gonna give your God a chance. I'm gonna give him a chance to save your black ass.

(CUTLER *crosses to below the lockers.* LEVEE *chases* CUTLER *to right of the upstage center bench.* SLOW DRAG *picks up the downstage left chair and crosses to behind the piano.*)

TOLEDO. Come on, Levee...put that knife up!

LEVEE. (*He swings the knife towards* TOLEDO. TOLEDO *steps quickly away downstage.*) Stay out of this, Toledo!

TOLEDO. That ain't no way to solve nothing.

LEVEE. (*Turns to* CUTLER *as* CUTLER *crosses to the piano and picks up the piano chair.*) I'm calling Cutler's God! I'm talking to Cutler's God! You hear me? Cutler's God! I'm calling Cutler's God. Come on and save this nigger!

(LEVEE *crosses above the upstage center bench toward* CUTLER *and swings the knife as* CUTLER *holds the chair out defensively and backs downstage right.*)

Strike me down before I cut his throat!

(LEVEE *chases* CUTLER *right around the downstage right bench.* CUTLER *backs to above the upstage center bench.*)

SLOW DRAG. Watch him, Cutler! Put that knife up, Levee!

LEVEE. (LEVEE *follows* CUTLER *to above the upstage center bench as* CUTLER *backs down toward the piano.*) I'm calling your God! I'm gonna give him a chance to save you! I'm calling your God! We gonna find out whose God he is!

CUTLER. (*Backs into the corner downstage left of the piano and holds the chair out toward* LEVEE.) You gonna burn in hell, nigger!

LEVEE. *(Looks upward.)* Cutler's God! Come on and save this nigger! Come on and save him like you did my mama! Save him like you did my Mama! I heard her when she called you! I heard her when she said, "Lord have mercy! Jesus help me! Please God have mercy on me, Lord! Jesus help me!" And did you turn your back? Did you turn your back, motherfucker? Did you turn your back? *(Stabs at the air above his head; frantically:)* Come on! Come on and turn your back on me! Turn your back on me! Come on! Where is you? Come on and turn your back on me! Turn your back on me, motherfucker! I'll cut your heart out! Come on, turn your back on me! Come on! What's the matter? Where is you? Come on and turn your back on me! Come on, what you scared of? Turn your back on me! Come on! Coward, motherfucker! *(Lowers the knife and looks around the room, closes the knife, slips it into his pants pocket and turns to* **CUTLER***; grins sardonically.)* Your God ain't shit, Cutler.

> *([Lights: Both rooms plunge into darkness. Sound: solo trumpet wails a long phrase, then* **MUSIC:** *the band plays* **"HEAR ME TALKING TO YOU."**])*

MA RAINEY. *(Singing.)*
HEAR ME TALKING TO YOU,
I DON'T BITE MY TONGUE.

> *([Lights: Studio lights come up brightly. The recording light is on.]* **MA,** *standing on the platform with a bottle of Coke in one hand and the feather fan in the other, sings into her mic.* **TOLEDO** *is sitting on the piano stool, playing the Studio piano,* **CUTLER** *is downstage left of* **TOLEDO,** *playing the guitar.* **SLOW DRAG** *is right of the piano, playing the bass.* **LEVEE** *is right of* **SLOW DRAG** *playing the cornet.* **DUSSIE MAE** *is sitting on the downstage right stool and* **SYLVESTER** *is sitting on the upstage left stool.* **STURDYVANT** *and* **IRVIN** *watch from the Control Booth.* **SYLVESTER***'s*

*mic is in the upstage right corner. **MA** waves the feather fan.)*

YOU WANT TO BE MY MAN,
YOU GOT TO FETCH IT WITH YOU WHEN YOU COME.

*([**MUSIC:** The song ends.] Everyone is silent as **STURDYVANT** lifts the recording needle.)*

IRVIN. *(Enthusiastically.)* Good! Wonderful! We have that, boys. Good session. That's great, Ma. We've got ourselves some winners.

*(He flips the recording light switch to off [Lights: The recording light goes off.] **CUTLER** turns to the guitar case, opens it, puts the guitar in it and closes the case.)*

TOLEDO. *(Relieved.)* Well, I'm glad that's over.

MA RAINEY. *(Crosses to downstage left of **TOLEDO**.)* Slow Drag, where you learn to play the bass at? You had it singing! I heard you! Had that bass jumping all over the place.

SLOW DRAG. *(Steps toward **MA**.)* I was following Toledo. Nigger got them long fingers…striding all over the piano. I was trying to keep up with him.

TOLEDO. That's what you supposed to do, ain't it? Play the music. Ain't nothing abstract about it.

MA RAINEY. *(Turns to **CUTLER**.)* Cutler, you hear Slow Drag on that bass? He make it do what he want it to do! Spank it just like you spank a baby.

CUTLER. Don't be telling him that. Nigger's head get so big his hat won't fit him.

SLOW DRAG. If Cutler tune that guitar up…we would really have something!

CUTLER. You wouldn't know what a tuned up guitar sounded like if you heard one.

TOLEDO. Cutler was talking. I heard him moaning. He was all up in it.

*(**LEVEE** looks expectantly at **MA**.)*

MA RAINEY. Levee…what is that you was doing?

(**LEVEE** *steps toward* **MA**.)

Why you playing all them notes? You play ten notes for every one you supposed to play. It don't call for that.

LEVEE. You supposed to improvise on the theme. That's what I was doing.

MA RAINEY. *(Sternly.)* You supposed to pay the song the way I sing it. The way everybody else play it. You ain't supposed to go off by yourself and play what you want.

LEVEE. I was playing the song. I was playing it the way I felt it.

MA RAINEY. I couldn't keep up with what was going on. I'm trying to sing the song and you up there messing up my ear. That's what you was doing. Call yourself playing music.

LEVEE. *(Crosses right and turns his back to* **MA**.) Hey... I know what I'm doing. I know what I'm doing, alright. I know how to play music. You all back up and leave me alone about my music.

CUTLER. I done told you...it ain't about your music. It's about Ma's music.

MA RAINEY. That's alright, Cutler. *(Crosses to the right folding chair and sits.)* I done told you what to do. *(Taking off her slippers.)*

LEVEE. I don't care what you do. You supposed to improvise on the theme. Not play note for note, the same thing over and over again.

(**CUTLER** *picks up* **MA***'s shoes and hands them to her.*)

MA RAINEY. *(Putting on her shoes.)* You just better watch yourself. You hear me?

LEVEE. *(Turns to* **MA**.) What I care what you or Cutler do? Come telling me to watch myself. What's that supposed to mean?

MA RAINEY. *(Warning.)* Alright...you gonna find out what it means.

LEVEE. *(Insolently.)* Go ahead and fire me. I don't care. I'm gonna get my own band anyway.

MA RAINEY. You keep messing with me.

LEVEE. Ain't nobody studying you. You ain't gonna do nothing to me. Ain't nobody gonna do nothing to Levee.

MA RAINEY. *(Sharply.)* Alright, nigger…you fired!

LEVEE. *(He looks at* **DUSSIE MAE***. She looks at the floor. He turns back to* **MA***.)* You think I care about being fired? I don't care nothing about that. You doing me a favor.

MA RAINEY. Cutler, Levee's out! He don't play in my band no more!

LEVEE. I'm fired…good! Best thing that ever happened to me. *(Crosses to the left door.)* I don't need this shit!

> *(Swings the left door open and exits into the Back Hall [Lights: The Band-room lights fade up.])*

MA RAINEY. *(Picks up her purse, rises and crosses to the double doors.)* Cutler, I'll see you back at the hotel.

> *(She goes through the double doors and gets her coat and* **DUSSIE MAE***'s coat.* **LEVEE** *opens the bandroom door, enters, crosses to the upstage center bench and sits.* **IRVIN** *and* **STURDYVANT** *leave the Control Booth.* **IRVIN** *opens the drape and crosses down the spiral stairs, followed by* **STURDYVANT***.)*

IRVIN. *(Crosses to downstage right of the piano as* **STURDYVANT** *goes through the double doors and exits up the front hall.)* Okay, boys…you can pack up. I'll get your money for you.

CUTLER. *(Crosses to* **IRVIN***.)* That's cash money, Mr. Irvin. I don't want no check.

> *(***TOLEDO** *crosses through the left door into the Back Hall, followed by* **SLOW DRAG***, carrying his bass.)*

IRVIN. I'll see what I can do. I can't promise you nothing.

CUTLER. *(Doggedly.)* As long as it ain't no check. I ain't got no use for a check.

IRVIN. I'll see what I can do, Cutler.

> *(He turns away from* **CUTLER** *as* **MA** *comes through the double doors. She drops* **DUSSIE MAE***'s coat onto her lap.* **IRVIN** *crosses to* **MA.** **CUTLER** *picks up the guitar case and the trombone and exits through the left door into the back hall.* **TOLEDO** *opens the bandroom door and enters, followed by* **SLOW DRAG.** **TOLEDO** *crosses to the piano, sits, picks up his newspaper and reads.* **SLOW DRAG** *crosses to behind the piano, puts down his bass, then crosses to the lockers.* **IRVIN** *helps* **MA** *on with her coat.)*

Oh, Ma, listen, I talked to Sturdyvant, and he said... now, I tried to talk him out of it...he said the best he can do is take twenty-five dollars of your money and give it to Sylvester.

MA RAINEY. *(Turns to* **IRVIN,** *incredulous.)* Take what and do what?

> *(***SYLVESTER*** *rises.* **CUTLER** *enters the bandroom, closes the door, puts his guitar case left of the lockers, crosses to the downstage right bench and sits.)*

Irvin, you better go and talk to him! If I wanted the boy to have twenty-five dollars of my money, I'd give it to him! He supposed to get his own money. He's supposed to get paid like everybody else. And you go on up there and tell Sturdyvant he better pay the boy his own money.

IRVIN. Ma... I talked to him...he said...

MA RAINEY. Go talk to him again! Tell him if he don't pay that boy...he'll never make another record of mine again. Tell him that! You supposed to be my manager. Always talking about sticking together. Start sticking! Go on up there and get that boy his money!

IRVIN. *(Crosses below* MA *to the double doors.)* Okay, Ma… I'll talk to him again. I'll see what I can do.

> *(He goes through the double doors and exits upstage the Front Hall. [Lights: The studio dims slightly as the bandroom brightens.]* MA *crosses and sits in the right folding chair.* SYLVESTER *sits in the left folding chair.)*

SLOW DRAG. *(Takes a deck of cards out of his pocket and crosses to upstage left of* LEVEE.*)* Come on, Levee, let me show you a card trick.

LEVEE. I don't want to see no card trick. What you wanna show me for? Why you wanna bother me with that?

SLOW DRAG. I was just trying to be nice.

LEVEE. *(Sulks.)* I don't need you to be nice to me. What I need you to be nice to be for? I ain't gonna be nice to you. I ain't even gonna let you be in my band no more.

SLOW DRAG. *(Crosses to behind the piano.)* Toledo…let me show you a card trick.

CUTLER. I just hope Mr. Irvin don't bring no check down here. What the hell I'm gonna do with a check?

SLOW DRAG. *(Fans the cards and holds them out toward* TOLEDO.*)* Alright, now…pick a card. Any card…go on…take any of them. I'm gonna show you something.

TOLEDO. *(Takes a card from the deck.)* I agrees with you, Cutler. I don't want no check either.

CUTLER. It don't make no sense to give a nigger a check.

SLOW DRAG. Okay, now. Remember your card. Remember which one you got. Now…put it back in the deck. Anywhere you want. I'm gonna show you something. *(*TOLEDO *glances at his card and slips it back into the deck.)* You remember your card? Alright. *(Crosses to right of* TOLEDO.*)* Now. I'm gonna shuffle the deck. *(Shuffles the deck a few times.)* Now… I'm gonna show you what card you picked. Don't say nothing, now. I'm gonna tell you what card you picked.

CUTLER. Slow Drag, that trick is as old as my mama.

SLOW DRAG. *(Turns to* **CUTLER.***)* Naw…naw…wait a minute! I'm gonna show him his card… *(Turns to* **TOLEDO,** *takes a card off the top of the deck and holds it up, triumphantly.)* There it go! The six of diamonds. Ain't that your card? Ain't that it?

TOLEDO. Yeah, that's is…the six of diamonds.

SLOW DRAG. Told you! Told you I'd show him what it was!

> *(He slips the card back into the deck, looks proudly around the room as* **TOLEDO** *returns to his newspaper and* **LEVEE** *and* **CUTLER** *stare at the floor.* **SLOW DRAG** *turns dejectedly to the locker and puts the cards in his coat pocket.)*

STURDYVANT. *(Enters down the Front Hall, goes through the double doors and crosses to downstage right of the piano, followed by* **IRVIN,** *carrying a pen and two forms.)* Ma, is there something wrong? Is there a problem?

MA RAINEY. Sturdyvant, I want you to pay that boy his money.

> *(***SLOW DRAG** *crosses to behind the bandroom piano and puts the cover on the bass.)*

STURDYVANT. Sure, Ma. I got it right here. *(Takes a large roll of money from his pants pocket, counts several bills into* **IRVIN** *'s hand and puts the rest of the roll in his pocket.)* Two hundred for you and twenty-five for the kid, right? *(Turns to* **MA.***)* Irvin misunderstood me. It was all a mistake. Irv made a mistake.

MA RAINEY. A mistake, huh?

IRVIN. *(Crosses to above* **SYLVESTER** *and hands him twenty-five dollars.)* Sure, Ma. I made a mistake. He's paid, right? I straightened it out.

> *(He crosses to right of* **MA** *and hands her two hundred dollars.* **SYLVESTER** *stares at the money in his hands, then puts it in his pocket.)*

MA RAINEY. The only mistake was when you found out I hadn't signed the release forms. That was the mistake! Come on, Dussie Mae. *(Rises, puts the money in her purse and crosses to the double doors.)*

STURDYVANT. Hey, Ma...come on, sign the forms, huh?

IRVIN. Ma...come on now.

MA RAINEY. Get your coat, Sylvester. *(Turns to **IRVIN**.)* Irvin, where's my car?

> *(**SYLVESTER** rises, picks up **MA**'s slippers, puts them in the bag, crosses through the double doors and gets his coat. **DUSSIE MAE** rises and puts on her coat.)*

IRVIN. It's right out front, Ma. Here... I got the keys right here. *(Takes the keys out of his pocket, crosses to **MA** and holds out the forms.)* Come on, sign the forms, huh?

> *(**SYLVESTER** puts on his coat.)*

MA RAINEY. Irvin, give me my car keys!

IRVIN. *(Hands the keys to **MA**.)* Sure, Ma...just sign the forms, huh?

MA RAINEY. Send them to my address and I'll get around to them.

> *(Turns to the double doors as **SYLVESTER** opens the upstage side of the double doors.)*

IRVIN. Come on, Ma... I took care of everything, right? I straightened everything out.

MA RAINEY. *(Turns back to **IRVIN**.)* Give me the pen, Irvin. *(Takes the pen and signs the papers in **IRVIN**'s hand, gives **IRVIN** the pen.)* You tell Sturdyvant...one more mistake like that and I can make my records someplace else. *(Turns toward the double doors and sees **SYLVESTER** in the doorway.)* Sylvester, straighten up your clothes. *(Sharply.)* Come on, Dussie!

> *(She crosses through the open double door and exits upstage the Front Hall, followed reluctantly by **DUSSIE MAE**. **SYLVESTER** plants his hat firmly on his head, nods at the men and follows **DUSSIE MAE**. The door swings shut as **IRVIN** turns to **STURDYVANT**. He taps the forms irritatedly, crosses to right of **STURDYVANT** and shoves the*

papers and the pen into **STURDYVANT**s *hand.*
IRVIN *crosses through the double doors into the*
Front Hall. He takes his hat and coat off the wall
hooks and puts them on. **STURDYVANT** *crosses to*
the piano, places the forms on the piano stool and
signs them. **SLOW DRAG** *crosses to the open locker.*)

CUTLER. *(Picks up the trombone case, puts it on the bench and*
opens it.) I know what's keeping him so long. He up
there writing out checks. You watch. I ain't gonna stand
for it. He ain't gonna bring me no check down here.
If he do, he's gonna take it right back upstairs and get
some cash. *(Disassembles the trombone and puts it in the*
case.)

TOLEDO. Don't get yourself all worked up about it. Wait
and see. Think positive.

CUTLER. I am thinking positive. He positively gonna give
me some cash. Man give me a check last time...you
remember...we went all over Chicago trying to get it
cashed. See a nigger with a check, the first thing they
think is he done stole it someplace.

LEVEE. I ain't had no trouble cashing mine.

CUTLER. I don't visit no whorehouses.

(**IRVIN** *comes through the double doors into the*
Studio, crosses to the left door and exits into the
Back Hall. **STURDYVANT** *follows after. [Lights:*
The Studio slowly dims.])

LEVEE. *(Rises and steps threateningly toward* **CUTLER.***)* You
don't know about my business. So don't start nothing.
I'm tired of you as it is. I ain't but two seconds off your
ass noway.

TOLEDO. Don't you all start nothing now.

CUTLER. What the hell I care what you tired of. I wasn't
even talking to you. I was talking to this man right here.

(**IRVIN** *opens the Bandroom door and crosses to*
behind the piano. **STURDYVANT** *enters and crosses*
to right of **TOLEDO.***)*

IRVIN. Okay, boys. Mr. Sturdyvant has your pay.

CUTLER. As long as it's cash money, Mr. Sturdyvant. 'Cause I have too much trouble trying to cash a check.

STURDYVANT. Oh, yes... I'm aware of that. Mr. Irvin told me you boys prefer cash, and that's what I have for you.

(He takes the roll of money out of his pocket and crosses to **CUTLER.** **SLOW DRAG** *crosses to right of the upstage center bench.)*

That was a good session you boys put in...that's twenty-five for you.

(Counts out twenty-five dollars and hands it to **CUTLER;** *he puts it in his pocket.)*

Yessir, you boys really know your business and we are going to...twenty-five for you...

(He turns to **SLOW DRAG,** *counts out twenty-five dollars and hands it to him.* **SLOW DRAG** *puts it in his pocket and crosses to the open locker.)*

We are going to get you back in here real soon... twenty-five...

(He turns to **LEVEE,** *counts out twenty-five dollars and hands it to him.* **LEVEE** *stuffs the money into his pants pocket.* **SLOW DRAG** *takes his coat out of the locker and puts it on.)*

And have another session so you can make some more money...and twenty-five for you.

(He crosses to right of **TOLEDO,** *counts out twenty-five dollars and hands it to him.* **TOLEDO** *puts the money in his jacket pocket.* **STURDYVANT** *turns toward* **CUTLER** *and puts the rest of the roll in his pants pocket.)*

Okay, thank you, boys. You can get your things together and Mr. Irvin will make sure you find your way out.

IRVIN. I'll be out front when you get your things together, Cutler.

(He crosses to the Bandroom doorway;
STURDYVANT *starts to follow.)*

LEVEE. Mr. Sturdyvant, sir. About them songs I give you?

STURDYVANT. *(Stops and turns to* **LEVEE.***)* Oh, yes...uh...
Levee. About them songs you gave me. I've thought
about it and I just don't think the people will buy
them...they're not the type of songs we're looking for.

(Starts toward the Bandroom door as **IRVIN** *exits
into the Back Hall.)*

LEVEE. Mr. Sturdyvant, sir...

*(***STURDYVANT** *stops again and turns back to*
LEVEE.*)*

I done got my band picked out and they's real good
fellows. They knows how to play real good. I know if
the peoples hear the music, they'll buy it.

STURDYVANT. Well, Levee... I'll be fair with you...but
they're just not the right songs.

*(***IRVIN** *comes through the left door, passes through
the Studio to the double doors. He goes through the
double doors and exits upstage the Front Hall.)*

LEVEE. Mr. Sturdyvant, you got to understand about the
music. That music is what the peoples is looking for.
They're tired of jug band music. They want something
that excites them. Something with some fire to it.

STURDYVANT. *(Crosses to left of* **LEVEE.***)* Okay, Levee. I'll tell
you what I'll do. I'll give you five dollars apiece for
them. Now, that's the best I can do.

LEVEE. *(Querulously.)* I don't want no five dollars, Mr.
Sturdyvant. I wants to record them songs like you say.

STURDYVANT. Well, Levee, like I say...they just aren't the
kind of songs we're looking for.

LEVEE. *(Restrained.)* Mr. Sturdyvant, you asked me to write
them songs. Now, why didn't you tell me that before
when I first give them to you? You told me you was
gonna let me record them. What's the difference
between then and now?

STURDYVANT. Well, look... I'll pay you for your trouble...

LEVEE. *(Insistently.)* What's the difference, Mr. Sturdyvant? That's what I wanna know.

STURDYVANT. *(Crosses to downstage right of the piano.)* I had my fellows play your songs...and when I heard them... They just didn't sound like the kind of songs I'm looking for right now.

LEVEE. *(Crosses to right of* **STURDYVANT.***)* You got to hear me play them, Mr. Sturdyvant! You ain't heard me play them. That's what's gonna make them sound right.

STURDYVANT. *(Crosses below* **LEVEE** *to left of* **CUTLER.***)* Well, Levee, I don't doubt that really. It's just that...well, I don't think they'd sell like Ma's records. But I'll take them off your hands for you.

LEVEE. *(Crosses to right of* **TOLEDO.***)* Mr. Sturdyvant, sir. I don't know what fellows you had playing them songs... but if I could play them! I'd set them down in the peoples lap! Now, you told me I could record them songs!

STURDYVANT. *(Dismissively.)* Well, there's nothing I can do about that. *(Takes a roll of money from his pants pocket.)* Like I say, it's five dollars apiece. That's what I'll give you. *(Counts out three five dollar bills and puts the rest of the money in his pocket.)* I'm doing you a favor. Now, if you write any more, I'll help you out and take them off your hands. The price is five dollars apiece. Just like now.

> *(He holds out the money and waits for* **LEVEE** *to take it.* **LEVEE** *stares blankly as* **STURDYVANT** *crosses to right of* **LEVEE** *and stuffs the money in* **LEVEE**'s *breast pocket.* **STURDYVANT** *crosses to the Bandroom door, exits and closes the door as* **LEVEE** *springs toward the door and puts his hand on his back pocket.* **LEVEE** *leans against the closed door for a moment, then crosses to right of* **TOLEDO.***)*

> CUTLER *closes his trombone case, rises and carries it to below the lockers.* SLOW DRAG *puts on his hat and crosses above* LEVEE *to behind the piano.* CUTLER *sets down the trombone case, opens his locker, takes out his coat and puts it on.* TOLEDO *rises, takes his coat off the piano and puts it on.* LEVEE *takes the money out of his breast pocket stares at it and turns toward the Bandroom door.* TOLEDO *reaches for his hat, puts it on and turns upstage as* LEVEE *curses silently, whirls downstage and collides with* TOLEDO.)

LEVEE. Hey! Watch it...shit! You stepped on my shoe! *(Crumples the money in his hand, throws it upstage right, crosses right and looks down at his shoe.)*

TOLEDO. Excuse me there, Levee.

LEVEE. *(Points at his shoe; angrily:)* Look at that! Look at that! Nigger, you stepped on my shoe. What you do that for?

TOLEDO. I said I'm sorry.

LEVEE. *(Enraged.)* Nigger gonna step on my goddamn shoe! You done fucked up my shoe! Look at that! Look at what you done to my shoe, nigger! I ain't stepped on your shoe! What you wanna step on my shoe for?

CUTLER. *(Crosses to upstage right of* TOLEDO.)* The man said he's sorry.

LEVEE. *(Crosses to the downstage right bench, puts his foot on the bench and unties his shoe.)* Sorry! How the hell he gonna be sorry after he done ruint my shoe? Come talking about sorry! *(Takes off his shoe and crosses to right of* TOLEDO.)* Nigger, you stepped on my shoe! You know that! *(Waves the shoe in* TOLEDO's *face.)* See what you done?

TOLEDO. *(Earnestly.)* What you want me to do about it? It's done now. I said excuse me.

LEVEE. Wanna go and fuck up my shoe like that. I ain't done nothing to your shoe. Look at this!

> *(*TOLEDO *turns toward the Bandroom door.* LEVEE *grabs* TOLEDO *by the arm and turns him back.)*

Naw...naw...look what you done! Look at that! That's
my shoe! Look at that! You did it! *(Throws the shoe
upstage left; furiously:)* You did it! You fucked up my
shoe! You stepped on my shoe with them raggedy-ass
clodhoppers!

TOLEDO. *(Exasperated.)* Nigger, ain't nobody studying you
and your shoe! I said excuse me. If you can't accept
that...then the hell with it. What you want me to do?
(Turns to the piano and picks up the book and newspaper.)

LEVEE. *(Reaches into his back pocket, takes out the pocket-knife,
opens it, lunges toward TOLEDO and stabs him in the back.)*
Nigger, you stepped on my shoe!!

> *(TOLEDO groans and falls backwards into
> LEVEE's arms. LEVEE quickly lowers TOLEDO's
> body to the floor, crosses upstage center and drops
> the knife. [Lights: The Band room slowly dims.]
> CUTLER crosses to above TOLEDO, kneels and
> touches TOLEDO's neck. LEVEE turns to CUTLER,
> shocked.)*

He...he stepped on my shoe. He did. Honest. Cutler,
he stepped on my shoe. What he do that for?

> *(CUTLER rises and crosses to upstage left, shaking
> his head. LEVEE turns to TOLEDO. Remorsefully:)*

Toledo, what you do that for?

> *(LEVEE crosses to TOLEDO's body, kneels and pulls
> at TOLEDO's arm, turns to CUTLER.)*

Cutler...help me. He stepped on my shoe, Cutler.
(Turns back to TOLEDO.) Toledo! Toledo, get up! *(Tries to
lift TOLEDO.)* It's okay, Toledo. Come on, stand up now.
Levee'll help you.

> *(TOLEDO's body slips out of LEVEE's hands and
> falls heavily to the floor. LEVEE lifts the limp body
> by the shoulders and looks into TOLEDO's open
> eyes.)*

Don't look at me like that! Toledo! *(Drops* **TOLEDO,** *stands and glares down at the body.)* Nigger, don't look at me like that! I'm warning you, nigger! *(Backs away to upstage center.)* Close your eyes! Don't you look at me like that! *(Turns to* **CUTLER***; whimpering:)* Tell him to close his eyes, Cutler. Tell him don't look at me like that.

CUTLER. Slow Drag...get Mr. Irvin down here.

*(***SLOW DRAG*** *crosses to the Bandroom door, opens it and exits into the Back Hall. [Sound: A trumpet begins to play a low, wailing solo. Lights: The stage begins to fade slowly.]* **CUTLER** *looks at* **LEVEE,** *shakes his head sadly and sits on the upstage center bench. [Sound: The trumpet builds in intensity and pitch and hits a high final note as, [Lights: The stage fades to black.])*

End of Play

PROPERTY PLOT

ON STAGE

FRONT HALL
Framed phonograph records (3)
Coat hooks

STUDIO
Framed phonograph record
"No smoking" sign
Large clock
Horn speaker on wooden wall mount
Piano on wooden platform
Singer's wooden platform
Music stands (2)
Cane chair (1)
Wooden folding chairs (4)
Wooden stools (3)
Radiator
Curtains
Jack boxes
Framed phonograph discs (2)

CONTROL BOOTH
On Counter:
    Desk microphone
    Recording machine
    Amplifier
    2 Headsets
On Shelves:
    Mixer
    Desk microphone phonograph records
    Files
    Gooseneck lamp
On Wall:
    Small clock
    Bulletin board with various papers
    Clipboard with various papers
    Stool
    Carpet
    Small electric fan

BANDROOM
Benches (2)
Cane chairs (2)
Folding chair

Piano
Ashtray (on piano)
Bucket & mop
Framed posters
Lockers fan (electric)
Crates (2)
Mirror—full length
Drum cases (2) small & large
Cymbal
Hi-hat with one cymbal
Music stands (2)
Ladder –"A"–5'
Recording horn on a stand Matches (on stand)
Fire extinguisher (on wall)

CLOSET
Microphones (2) on stands
Crate of empty Coke bottles
Guitar—no case

OFF-RIGHT

STURDYVANT:
Levee's song sheet
Recording discs wrapped in paper (5)
Large roll of paper money

IRVIN
Small piece of paper (list of songs)
Pen
Release forms
Car keys
8 Dollar bills

CUTLER
Trombone case with:
    Trombone
    Tobacco pouch with tobacco
    Rolling paper
    Spray bottle with water
    Rag
Guitar case
Box of matches
"Reefer"

TOLEDO
Newspaper
Book
2 Dollar bills

Small cardboard box with:
    5 Sandwiches wrapped in wax paper (Daily)

SLOW DRAG
Bass case with:
    Bass
Bottle of bourbon (full)—pint
Deck of cards
Small paper bag with:
    Three bottles of Coke
    Bottle opener

LEVEE
Cornet case with:
    Silver-plated cornet
    Rag
    Music manuscript paper (3) with songs
    Pencil
Florsheim shoebox with:
    New shoes wrapped in tissue paper
Pocket knife
2 Dollar bills

MA RAINEY
Purse (wardrobe)
A single dollar bill (in purse)

DUSSIE MAE
Purse (wardrobe)
Nailfile (kept in purse)
Doublemint gum

SYLVESTER
A Large loop-handled bag with:
    Ma's slippers
    Large feather fan

POLICEMAN
Nightstick

PROPERTY RUNNING NOTES

PRE-SHOW SET:

All Studio and Bandroom doors closed
Clock (over piano)—set to 12:55 at Estimated Curtain Time
Guitar is *not in case*
Bourbon bottle:
    Instant iced tea (refill daily)—pint
Sandwiches:
    Peanut Butter and Jelly on bread (five, wrapped in wax paper, each
        performance)
Cokes:
    Coke in small glass Coke bottles (one is opened and consumed each
        performance)

INTERMISSION SCENE SHIFT:

Strike sandwich box
Strike bass, trombone, guitar case, cornet (to off-stage upstage center)
Close Studio door and Bandroom door

ACT TWO INTERIOR SHIFT:

Strike Sylvester's mic from closet to offstage right (after it is replaced
    there by Irvin)
In Blackout Transition:
    Hand-off guitar to Cutler (through Studio left door)
    Reset clock ahead four hours (approx. 3:30 to 7:30) COSTUME
    PLOT

STURDYVANT
Grey and mauve striped wool three piece suit
Blue check long-sleeved shirt with a white collar
Suspenders
Maroon polka dot bow tie
Brown lace-up shoes
Gold wedding band
Gold money clip
Handkerchief

IRVIN
Dark grey three piece suit
Beige long-sleeved shirt
Grey with yellow patterned tie
Black lace-up shoes
Brown tweed wool overcoat
Brown felt fedora
Pocket watch and chain

Leather belt
Suspenders
Handkerchief
Silver frame eyeglasses

CUTLER
Black and white checked two piece suit
Terracotta long-sleeved shirt Suspenders
Red, black and off-white striped tie
Black lace-up shoes
Brown teddybear fur overcoat with a belt
Grey cap
Gloves
Handkerchief
Gold ring with an onyx stone
Gold tie pin

SLOW DRAG
Navy blue pinstriped three piece suit
Grey long-sleeved shirt
Blue and purple paisley print tie
Black lace-up shoes
Grey stormcoat with a beige fur collar
Brown tweed cap
Suspenders
Handkerchief
Diamond ring

TOLEDO
Grey and green striped three piece suit
Olive green striped long-sleeved shirt
Green silk tie
Dark brown and grey lace-up ankle boots
Beige cashmere overcoat
Grey homburg
Yellow leather gloves
Gold ring
Tie pin

LEVEE
Silver grey, blue and black striped two piece suit
Lilac long-sleeved shirt
Black and blue striped suspenders
Black vest
Black and pink tie
Black lace-up shoes
Yam lace-up shoes (new)
Black chesterfield overcoat with a velvet collar

Black felt fedora
Dark blue and cream print silk scarf
Handkerchief
Gold tie stud
Diamond ring

POLICEMAN
Navy blue uniform jacket with a badge
Navy blue uniform pants
Navy blue cap with a badge
Black shoes

MA RAINEY
Pink lamé, beaded dress
Wine silk chiffon, beaded kimono
Pink silk stockings
Maroon and gold pumps
Purple velvet hat with a feather
Silver lame headband with beaded tassels
Full-length racoon coat
Small alligator skin handbag
Purple and bronze slipper bag
Pink satin slippers
Wine ostrich feather fan
Long, beaded, metallic necklace
Rhinestone clip-on earrings
Three rings

DUSSIE MAE
Peach silk chiffon long-sleeve dress with a belt
Peach silk stockings
Silver leather pumps
Gold silk velvet coat with silver fox fur collar
Silk cut-velvet beaded purse
Black velvet cloche hat with pink silk flowers
Lead crystal pink and white necklace
Pink pearl necklace
Rhinestone clip-on earrings

SYLVESTER
Mauve two piece suit (unpressed)
Long sleeve peach shirt
Suspenders
Lime green silk tie
Black lace-up ankle boots
Brown felt fedora
Brown cashmere overcoat
Cufflinks

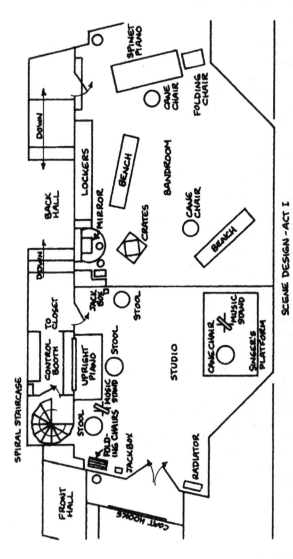

SCENE DESIGN – ACT I

"MA RAINEY'S BLACK BOTTOM"